New Kent County, Virginia

❖❖❖❖❖❖❖❖❖❖❖❖❖❖

U.S. Census for 1810
&
U.S. Census for 1850
&
Abstarcts of the Application Papers of the Revolutionary War Pensioners.

Volume #1

Southern Historical Press, Inc.

This volume was reproduced from
An 1938 edition located in the
Publisher's private library,
Greenville, South Carolina

All rights reserved. No part of this publication
may be reproduced, stored in a retrieval system,
transmitted in any form, posted on to the web
in any form or by any means without the
prior written permission of the publisher.

Please direct all correspondence and orders to:

www.southernhistoricalpress.com
or
SOUTHERN HISTORICAL PRESS, Inc.
PO BOX 1267
375 West Broad Street
Greenville, SC   29601
southernhistoricalpress@gmail.com

Originally published: Washington, D.C. 1938
Reprinted: Southern Historical Press, Inc.
Greenville, SC 2017
ISBN #0-89308-783-1
Printed in the United States of America

PREFACE.

In June 1936 it was brought to our attention by our good friends Miss Sally Whitcomb and Dr. Edward Thompson of the Martha Washington Seminary here in Washington, that the birthplace of Martha Washington was not known. Our chapter immediately undertook to locate the house, and of course wanted documentary proofs concerning it. The lack of any county records in New Kent prior to about 1780 when the Courthouse was burned, was a terrible handicap in this. After several months research, however, enough evidence was gotten from other sources to satisfy the committee that "Chestnut Grove" in that county was the right place. Consequently an appropriate marker was placed on this property by the chapter.

The house had a beautiful setting high on the banks of the Pamunkey River. It was spacious and interesting, but was of frame construction and unfortunately burned about 1928. The Martha Dandridge Womans' Club of New Kent County, some of the descendants of Martha, our Martha Washington Chapter and many patriotic persons are anxious to see the house and grounds restored and maintained as a memorial to this loveable and talented woman who exemplified everything that is good in a wife, mother, home-maker and patriotic woman of her time.

Therefore as our first enterprize toward this end, the Martha Washington chapter has started a ten year program of collecting and publishing records pertaining to the early residents of New Kent County, wherever they can be found; selling the publications and contributing the proceeds to the fund for the restoration. We submit here volume one of this project, which contains the first U. S. Census of New Kent that is extant-(the British having burned the 1790 and 1800 census of Va.) and the 1850 census which is the first one that gives the name of every inhabitant of the county. With those we give the abstracts of the applications papers of Revolutionary Pensioners of New Kent, picking out all genealogical data and every name that is mentioned. If this volume is a financial success, the chapter will continue to collect and publish until several volumes have been brought out and can be bound together making quite a large book of New Kent Records.

We have copied these records carefully and have given all spellings as we found them, such as: "Newport nuse" and "Tumbul cart", "plough" and "skedule". We are happy to be doing this work for the dual purpose: making available the genealogical material for the county,-- and helping restore the Dandridge home.

Our announcement of this undertaking has been so encouragingly received by genealogists and those interested in the county, that we must here express our gratitude to them for their valuable suggestions and help. To Mrs. Annie Walker Burns, who is giving the labor in connection with the mimeographing of this volume absolutely free of charge, and who presented the chapter with a typed copy of the 1810 census which she had made for herself,-- in her desire to help with this worthy cause, we give our sincere thanks.

The chapter members have cooperated in such a gratifying, generous manner that they too should be thanked here, especially those who helped so materially with the typing and contributed toward the purchase of the photostat copy of the 1850 census which will be bound and given to the Court House at New Kent. To our many friends and friendly strangers who will buy the books, we send our thanks and good wishes that we may all have the pleasure of visiting Chestnut Grove in a few years and seeing it in a beautifully restored condition.

Florence Bridges Culver, Regent of the
MARTHA WASHINGTON CHAPTER, N.S.D.A.R.

Page 1.

THIRD U. S. CENSUS
1810
NEW KENT COUNTY, VIRGINIA

Skedule of division allotted to Anthony Davis, Assistant.

NAMES	MALES Under 10	10 to 16	16 to 26	26 to 45	45 & up	FEMALES Under 10	10 to 16	16 to 26	26 to 45	45 & up	FREE Black.	Slaves.
Anderson, John	1	0	0	1		0	0	0	1			1
Allen, James	2	1	2	0	1.	1	3	1	0			12
Acre, Sarah	0	0	1	0	0	0	1	2	0	1		1
Armistead, Robert B.	0	2	1	0	1	1	0	1				25
Apperson, Littleberry	1	1	0	0	1	5	1	0	0	1		
Allen, John G.	4	0	0	1	0	0	0	0	1			7.
Austin, John	2	2	0	1	0	1	1	0	1	1		4
Allen, Richard	0	1	1	0	0							45
Armistead, Wm												12
Apperson, Richard	0	1	2	0	1							7
Allen, James, Junr.	0	0	1									3
Adams, Epaphroditus	0	1	0	0	2	2	0	1	1			
Atkinson, James	1	1	0	1	0	1	0	1	1			5
Armistead, Guy											2	
Atkinson, Mary	2	1	0	0	0	1	1	0	1			19
Anderson, James	0	0	0	1	0	0	0					2
Amey											1	
Austin, Zachariah	2	1	0	1		1 (paper torn)						2
Apperson, Folly	1	2	0	1		2	1	0	2			16
Austin, Richard	0	1	0	0	1	0	1	0	0	1		1
Ayres, C. John	0	0	0	1	0	0	1	0	0	0	1	1
Austin, Julius H	1	0	0	1	0	0	0	1	0	1		
Adams, John												18
Ashwell, Mary						0	0	0	0	0	3	2
Adams, Peter	0	0	0	0	1	0	0	0	0	1		2
Apperson, William	0	0	2	0	1	0	0	1	1	1		9
Apperson, Edmund	1	0	2	1	0	0	0	1	0			20
Allen, William	0	0	1	0	0	0						1
Boyd, Robert	1	2	1	0	1	0	0	0	0	1		30
Boyd, William	0	0	1	0	0	0	0	1				12
Baker, Richard	0	1	0	1	1	0	0	1	0	1		1
Berlimeyer, John O.	0	0	0	1		0						1
Betty _____?											1	
Binns, Charles	0	0	1	0	0							
Boswell, William	2	0	0	1	0	1	1	0	1	0		1
Bailey, William	0	0	0	0	2	0	1	1	0	1	2	22
Birch, Milley	0	0	0	1	0							1
Birch, Mary	2	0	1	0	0	0	0	1	2	0		9

Page 2-

Bradley, Anne	0	0	0	0	0		0	1	1	0	1	0	1
Braxton, Abram												5
Bird, Sam												1
Brookes, Sam												1
Bodkins, Sally	0	1	0	1								3
Birch, Reuben	2	1	0	1			1	0	0	1		1
Bailey, Jane	1	0	0	1			0	0	0	1		
Barkwell, Thomas	0	1	0	1	0		2	0	0	1		10
Bailey, Anselm, Jr	1	3	0	1	0		1	0	0	1		2
Binns, Jeremiah	0	0	0								1	
Bowers, John	1	0	0	1	0		2	0	1	0	0	10
Bassett, Burwell												96
Bradenham, Robert	0	1	1	0	1		0	2	1	0	2	13
Bone, Hezekiah	0	0	0	1	0		2	0				5
Bailey, James	1	1	0	1	0		1	0	0	1		
Bailey, Samuel	0	1	1	0	1		0	0	2	0	1	20
Binns, Daniel	1	0	0	1	0		1	0	0	1		11
Bailey, Anselmn, Sr.	0	0	2	0	1		0	1	0	0	1	
Binns, David	0	0	0	0	1		1	1	0	0	1	
Binns, Martha	0	2	1	0	0		0	0	1	0	1	5	1
Binns, Marston	0	0	0	1	0		0	0	0	1		1
Baker, John												8
Brewell, William	2	0	0	0	0		1	1	0	1		
Ball, Parkes	1	0	0	1	0		2	1	0	1		
Bradley, Edward	0	0	1	2	0							1
Barker, Salley	0	1					0	0	0	0	1	
Barker, John	0	0	1	0	1		0	0	1	0	1	1
Bailey, William Capt.	1	0	2	0	1		1	1	0	1		9
Binns, John	0	0	0	1	0							5
Bosman, James											7	
Bowis, Wm	1	1	0	1			1	1	0	1		11
Binns, Jeremiah, Jr							0	0	0	1	6	1
Bosman, Benskin											4	
Baker, Richard	0	0	1	1	1		0	0	1	0	1	1
Breeding, Julius	1	0	0	1	0		3	0	1	0		1
Breeding, John	0	0	1	0	1		0	1	0	0	1	1
Ball, George	0	0	2	0	1		0	0	1	0	1	8
Bowis, Scott, Jesse	1	0	0	1	0		2	0	0	1		1
Bailey, William, Jr.	3	0	0	1			2	1	0	2		
Bradley, Pleasant	0	1	1	1	0		1	0	0	1		12
Boswell, John	1	0	1	0	0		0	1	1			
Binns, Richard	0	0	0	1	0							2
Brown, John	1	0	1	0	0		0	1	1	1		
Bacon, Elizabeth							0	1	0	0	1	6
Benford, Robert												4
Benford, George											1	
Carlo, John, Jr	0	0	0	1	0		3	0	1			2
Clopton, John	0	0	2	0	1		0	2	0	0	1	1	29
Clopton, James	0	0	0	1	0		0	0	1			5
Cosby, John	0	1	0	1	0		2	0	0	1	0	4
Crump, Jesse	1	1	2	0	1		0	1	2	0	1	16
Crump, Josiah	0	2	0	1	0		0	1	0	1	1	45
Crump, Edmund	2	0	0	1	0		1	0	1	0		9
Crump, Thomas	1	0	0	1	0		0	0	1	1		6
Crump, Christopher	0	2	1	0	1		1	0	1			21

Chopeland, Michael	0										6	1
Crawley, William	0	0	2	0	0	0	0	0	0	0		1
Clopton, Wm (B)	0	0	0	0	2	0	2	1	1	1		18
Clopton, John Sr.	0	0	0	0	1	0	0	1	1	0		7
Crump, Anne	1	1	2	1		0	0	3	0	1		18
Christian, Robert	2	1	1	0	1	1	3	2	0	1		40
Crump, Nathaniel	4	0	0	1	0	0	0	0	1			31
Crump, Abner	1	0	0	1		0	0	1				6
Crump, John	0	0	1	0	0	0	0	1	0	1		11
Curle, David	0	0	2	1	0	0	0	1	0	1		10
Carter, John	1	0	1	1		3	0	0	1	1		25
Crump, Richard	3	0	0	1	0	3	0	0	1	1		
Clopton, Wm. R.	0	0	0	0	1	0	0	1	0	1		10
Crump, William	1	0	4	0	1	0	0	1	0	1		21
Crump, George	3	0	0	1	0	2	2	1	1			4
Clarke, William	0	0	1	0	0	0	0	1				
Crump, James	0	0	0	1								
Cambo, Nelson	0	0	0	1	0	0	0	0	0	1		
Curle, Richardson	0	0	1			1	0	1	0			2
Clarke, John	3	0	1	1	0	1	1	0	1			
Crump, Richard	0	0	1	0	0							5
Crump, Anderson	0	0	0	1	0	1	0	0	2			7
Crump, John P.	0	2	1	0	1	1	2	2	1			14
Clarke, David	0	0	0	0	1	0	0	1	1	1		
Crittenden, Sally	3	0	0	0	0	0	0	0	1			1
Chappel, Benjamin	0	0	1	1	1	0	1	2	0	1		9
Clopton, Waldergrave	2	2	1	0	1	0	2	1	0	1		17
Crump, John C.	0	0	1	0	0	0	1	0	0	0	1	37
Claiborne, Thomas	1	1	1	1		1	1	0	3	0		78
Chamberlayne, Wm.	2	3	1	0	1	1	1	2	1	1		101
Custis, Geo.W.P.											1	3
Crutchfield, John												
Chandler, Thomas B.	1	1	2	0	1	0	1	1	1			
Crump, Will											6	
Crow, Anthony	1	1	0	0	1	0	1	1	1			
Cockerham, Edward	0	0	0	1	0	3	1	0	1			
Clayton, William B.	2	1	1	1		1	1				4	29
Chappel, Winchester	1	0	1	0	0	1	0	1	0		1	
Clopton, Edwin												5
Crow, James	0	0	0	1		1	1	1				1
Crump, Beverley	3	0	0	1	0	0	0	0	1			8
Crump, Benedict	0	0	0	0	1	0	0	1	0	1		12
Curle, Benet	3	1	0	1	0	1	0	1	1			
Crow, Jesse	0	0	0	0	1	0	0	1	0	1		
Cosby, Charles	1	0	0	1	0	3	0	0	1			9
Christian, Agness											1	5
Clarke, Jesse	0	1	0	1	0	2	0	1	1			
Chandler, Richard	0	0	1	0	0	0	0	1	0			8
Chandler, William	1	1	1	1	0	1	0	1				11
Cooper, Jesse											7	
Christian, Archer	0	0	0	1	0	4	0	2	0			18
Christian, Collier	0	1	2	2	0	0	0	0	0	1		28
Christian, John H.	0	0	1	1	0	0	2	0	0			30
Christian, Gideon	0	0	1								1	17
Christian, Jones, R.	1	0	2	1	0	0	1	0				21

Curle, John	0	0	0	0	1		0	1	0	0	1	20
Clarke, Charles	2	1	0	1	0		1	0	1			
Chandler, James	3	1	1	0	1		1	0	0	0	1	7
Cook, William	0	0	0	1			0	0	0	0	1	6
Douglas, William	3	0	1	1	0		0	0	0	1	1	68
Dennet, James	0	1	0	1	0		1	1	2	1		5
Dow, Robert	1	1	1	0	0		1	0	0	1		4
Dixon, Edward	2	2	0	0	1		2	2	2			7
Davis, Anthony	0	1	0	0	1		1	1	1	2		3
Dennett, Catharine	1	0	1	0			1	0	2	1	1	5
Dobson, Richard	0	0	1	1	1		0	1	1	1	1 1	11
Dennett, Richard	2	0	0	1			1	0	1			3
Daniel, Parke	1	1	0	0	1		1	2	1			
Dandridge, Bartholo--mew	1	0	0	1			1	0	1			9
Drinkard, William												14
Dungey, Reuben											7	
Davis, John	1	0	0	1			2	0	0	1		
Day, Wm. W.	0	0	1									
Dillard, Edward	0	1	1	0	1							12
Diggs, Isaac	3	2	0	1	0		1	0	1			10
Dangey, Isabella											4	
Ellyson, Jesse	1	0	0	1			4	0	0	1		
Easter, Sally	0						1	2	0	1		12
Ellyson, Margaret	0	0	1				0	0	0	1		1
Banes, John, Sr.	0	1	3	0	1							4
Banes, William	2	0	0	1			0	0	1			1
Ellyson, Jonathan	0	0	0	1			3	0	0	1		2
Ellyson, Agness	0	0	1				0	0	0	3	1 1	
Ellyson, Gideon	1	2	0	0	1		0	0	1	0	1	
Eggman, Christopher	0	0	0	1	0		2	0	0	1		16
Eames, Joel	1	1	0	1			0	0	1	0	1 2	1
Evans, James	0	0	0	1	0		1	0				
Ellyson, David											2	
Ellyson, Sam											3	
Eames, John, Jr	1	2	0	1	0		1	0	0	1	1	7
Foster, Jesse											4	
Farris, Sylvanus	0	0	1	0	1							1
Farris, John			1		1		0	0	0	1		2
Farris, Wm	0	0	0	1			1	0	0	1		
Fox, James											12	
Frayser, Elvira	1	1	1				(0	1	0	0	:1	15
Furgerson, Francis	2	2	0	0	1		1	1	0	0	1	8
Fields, John											4	
Franks, John	1	0	0	1			2	0	1			3
Finch, James	0	0	0	0	1		0	2	2	0	1	8
Frayser, Beverley	0	0	1									
Faris, Jacob	0	0	0	1			0	0	1			4
Furlong, Alexander	0	0	0	1			0	0	0	1	1	1
Frances, John	0	0	0	1			0	0	1	0	1	9
Fox, Nathaniel	0	0	0	1								
Finch, Samuel	0	0	0	1								
Foster, Joseph	0	0	0	1	2		0	0	0	1	2	31
Finch, Wm.	1	1	1	0	1		2	0	1	1	0 0	10

Page 4

Freeman, Sally	0	1	0	0	0	0	0	0	0	1	3	1
Firth, John	0	0	0	1		0	0					16
Firth, Samuel	0	0	0	1		1	0	1	0	1		6
Firbush, Thomas	0	0	1	0	0							
Glen, John	2	3	0	0	1							4
Gibson, Jeduthon	0	0	0	1		0	0	0	1			8
Geddy, William												9
Gennings, Sally	2	1	0			1	0	0	0	1		
Galling, Samuel	0	0	1	0	1	0	1	1	0	1		
Galling, Samuel, Jr.	1	0	1	0		0	0	0	1			
Goodman, Elizabeth	0	1	0	0		2	0	1	1	1		
Gathwright, Robert	0	0	0	1		1	0	0	1			3
George, Bird												9
Green, William	1	0	0	1		0	1	0	1			2
Gilliam, Epaphroditus	1	0	0	1		3	0	1				2
Gower, Stanley, P.	0	0	0	2		3	0	1	0	1		1
Geddin, Avery	1	1	1	0	1	0	2	3				14
Glass, David	0	0	0	1		0						
Glaisbrook, James, Jr	2	0	0	1		1	0	1				
Garnet, James	0	0	0	0	1	0	1	1	0	1		
Godfrey-											1	
Gregory, William	0	0	0	1		0	1	0	1			3
Graves, Richard	3	1	0	1		1	1	0	1			15
Graves, Edmund	1	0	0	1		2	0	0	1			10
Green, Edward	0	0	0	1								
Gary, James	1	1	1	1		3	1	1				7
Gilliam, Frances	3	0	0	0		0	0	0	1			
Howle, Charles	1	1	1	0	1	1	1	5	0	1		11
Holsworth, Elizabeth						0	0	0	2			1
Harman, Keziah	0	0	1	1	1						1	3
Harman, Elizabeth						0	0	2	0	1		6
Harman, Ishamar	3	1	2	0	1	1	1	2	1			8
Hamlet, Burwell	1	1	0	0	1	0	0	1			1	
Herbert, Anthony												6
Hix, William	3	1	0	0	1	1	0	0	2			
Howle, Mary	0	0	0	1		1						1
Howle, Daniel	2	2	1	1		2	2	0	1			6
Hill, John	1	0	0	0	1	1	1	0	1			
Hollins, Delphis	0	0	0	1							3	
Higgens, Josiah	0	0	1	2	0	1	0	1				3
Howle, John	1	0	0	1		2	0	1	1			1
Hopkins, Priscilla	1	2	0			0	0	1	1			6
Hilliard, John	0	0	1	1		0	0	0	0	1	1	8
Howle, Lewis	1	1	0	0	1	2	1	1	1	1	5	7
Hix, George	1	1	0	1		2	0	0	1			
Hilliard, Benskin, H	0	1	0	1	1	3	2	0	1			25
Hughes, Elizabeth	0	0	1			0	0	1	1		1	
Harman, John	1	0	0	1		1	1	0	1			1
Hix, Edward	3	1	0	1		1	0	1	1			1
Hilliard, Richard	1	1	1	1		1	1	0	2	1		9
Hockaday, Wm	2	1	1	0	1	1	2	1	1			11
Hilliard, Benskin	0	0	2	0		0	0	1	0		1	9
Hall, Richard	2	0	0	1		1	1	0	1			1

Name	C1	C2	C3	C4	C5	C6	C7	C8	C9	C10	C11
Harman, John Jr	2	0	0	1		2	1	0	0	0	2
Hix, Nathaniel	0	1	0	1		0	1	0	0	1	1
Hilliard, Mary	0	0	1			0	0	1	1	1	3
Howle, Thomas	3	0	0	1		0	0	0	1	1	1
Haslegrave, John	1	0	0	1		1	1	1			
Holt, William	0	0	0	1							
Haslegrave, Mary	0	1	1			0	0	2	0	1	
Higgens, Foster	1	2	1	1		3	1	0	1		3
Hockaday, Edmund	1	0	2	1		3	0	0	1		3
Hockaday, Sally	1	1				1	0	2	0	1	2
Hoomes, Amos										1	1
Hill, Parkes,	2	1	0	1		4	0	1			15
Howle, Gideon	0	0	0	0	1	0	0	0	1	1	8
Hix, John	0	0	1	0	1	1	1	0	0	1	
Howl, Isaac	0	0	1								
Halsey, Isaac	0	0	1	1		0	0	0	1		1
Hilliard, Thomas	2	0	0	1		-1	0	0	-1		
Halyburton, William	1	0	1	0	1	0	0	0	1		15
Hylton, John	0	0	1	0	1	0	2	3	0	1	8
Jordan & Douglas											45
Jeffery										2	
Jones, Robert	0	1	0	1		0	0	0	1		
Johnson, David										2	
Jones, Cillar										5	
Jones, Elizabeth						0	0	1	1	1	2
Jones, Nancy						0	0	1	0	1	3
Jones, Chesley	3	0	0	1		1	0	0	1		10
Ingram, Wm.G	0	2	0	1		1	0	0	1		4
Jackson, Aaron										1	
Jones, Nancy	1					0	1	0	0	1	2
Jones, Nelson	0	0	0	1		1	0	0	1		2
Jones, William	1	0	0	1		2	0	0	1		3
Jones, Edward	0	0	1			0	0	1			5
Jones, Charles	0	0	1			0	0	1			4
James, Ann	2	2	3			1	0	0	0	1	
Jones, William, Jr.	0	0	0	1		2	0	0	1		2
Jones, Robert.E.	0	0	0	1		0	0	0	1		
Johnson, William										25	5
Jones, Daniel	0	0	3	0	1	0	0	0	0	1	3
Jones, William	0	0	0	1							
Kilby, John T	0	0	1								
Keiningham, Benj	0	0	0	1		0	0	0	1		5
Knight, William	0	1	0	0	1	1	0	0	1		
Kent, William	0	2	2	0	1	0	0	1	1	1	
Kent, Thomas	1	0	1			0	0	2			
Keiningham, Samuel	1	0	0	1		2	0	0	2		
Lacy, Philemon	1	0	0	1		2	1	0	1		2
Lacy, Stephen	0	1	1			0					3
Lacy, Mary	2	1							1		
Layfayette, James										11	3
Lewis, Roger										1	3
Lindsey, John	0	0	0	0	1	0	3	1			1
Ladd, James	0	0	1			0	1	1			12

Page 7

Ladd, John	0	0	1			0	0				0	1
Lewis, Catey						0	0				3	
Lacy, William	1	0	0	1	1	0	0	1-				5
Lawson, William	0	0	0	1								
Lockhart, Samuel	1	2	0	1		0	0	0	1			1
Lacy, Bacon	1	0	0	1		0	0	1				
Langley, Henry B.	0	0	0	1		0	0	0	1		1	1
Lyon, William	0	0	0	1		1						
Langley, Wm	0	0	0	0	1	0	0	1				9
Langley, John W.	0	0	0	1		2	0	1				3
Ladd, William	0	2	1	0	1	0	1	2	1	1		5
Ladd, David	1	0	0	0	1	1	1	1	0	1		10
Lewis, Burnett												22
Lacy, Archibald	3	1	0	1		1	1	0	2			17
Martin, Julius	1	0	0	0	1	0	0	1				9
Martin, John S.	0	0	0	1		0	0	1				
Morris, Thomas	0	0	1								1	12
Meekins, Ned											6	
Mullin, John	0	0	0	0	1	0	0	1				6
Martin, Caleb	2	0	1	0		2	0	1	2			
Moss, George											3	
Morgan, Jane	1	0				0	2	0	1			5
Martin, Dandridge	2	0	0	1		0	0	0	1			1
Mahone, Richard	0	0	1			0	0	0	0	1		
Meekins, David											6	
Meekins, Joseph											3	
Meekins, Christmas											2	1
Moore, William	0	0	0	0	1	0	1	0	0	2	1	7
Martin, Elizabeth	0	1	0			1	0	0	1			
Moss, William	2	0	0	1		1						6
Mason, John	3	1	0	0	1	0	1	0	0	1		
Martin, Julius, Jr	0	0	1									
Massie, William	0	0	0	1								
Martin, William B.	0	0	1			1	0	1			1	2
Moore, Berned	0	0	0	1		0	0	0	1			
Morris, Daniel	0	0	0	2		0	0	1				2
Moody, Thomas	0	0	0	0	1	0	0	0	0	1		4
Moon, Christopher	1	0	0	1		3	0	0	1			9
Meekins, Isaac											9	
Moss, Samuel, Jr	1	0	0	0	1	0	0	0	1		5	
Moss, Julius											1	
Moss, Samuel	0	1	0	0	1	0	0	0	1	1		5
Moss, William	●	0	0	0	1	0	0	0	0	1		7
Mennin, William	0	0	1									3
Mennin, Richardson	1	0	0	1		1	0				1	
Meanly, Elizabeth	0	0	1			0	2	1	0	1	1	14
Moss, Judith	0	0	1	1		1	1	0	0	1		8
Meux, Hubbard, R	0	0	0	1		1	1	0	1			6
Martin, Ellyson	1	3	2	1		3	0	0	1			10
Martin, Joshua	2	0	0	1	1	0	0	1	1	1		1
Martin, Alice	0	0	0	1		1	0	0	1			
Meux, Thomas	0	0	1									4
McCarty, Loudon											1	1

Page 8

Morris, John	0	0				0	0			2	
Macon, Wm. H	0	1	0	2	1	1	0	1	1		88
Marry, William	2	0	0	0	1	2	0	1	2		
Mutlow, Zachariah											4
Miller, Christopher	2	0	3	1		0	0	0	1		4
McGrigger, John	2	1	0	1		0	1	1	0	1	
Morris, John C.	0	1	0	1		0	1	0	0		15
Mannin, Armistead	0	1	1								3
Moore, John A	1	2	1	1		1	1	1	1	1	8
Batts, Morris	1	0	0	1		1	2	0	1		
Massie, Hugh	0	0	0	1							9
Massie, Anne						0	0	0	1	1	18
Mercer, Elizabeth	0	1				0	0	0	2		5
Mannin, Richard	0	0	0	1							
Massie, John	1	0	1	0	1	2	1	0	1		10
Merryman, Thomas	0	1	0	1		2	0	0	1	3	
Martin, John	1	0	1	1		0	0	0	1		
Mills, John	1	0	2	0	1	0	0	1	0	1	1
Martin, Wm.	0	0	0	1		1	0	1	1		6
Martin, James	2	0	0	1	1	0	0	1	0	1	1
Martin, Joshua	0	1	0	2		2	0	0	1		3
Otey, Elizabeth	1	0	0	0		2	0	0	1		1
Osborne, Squire										4	1
Oakley, James	2	1	0	0	1	1	0	1	1	3	5
Otter, John G	0	1	0	0	1	1	0	1	1		7
Otey, James	3	0	0	1		2	0	0	1		
Otey, Marye Anne	0	2	1			1	1	0	1		1
Otey, Isaac	0	0	1			0	0	2			4
Owen, William	0	0	0	0	1	0	0	2	0	1	5
Pomfrey, Mildred	2	0				1	0	0	2		
Poindexter, Polly	0	0	1			0	0	2	0	1	15
Parsons, Hopewell	0	0	0	1		0	0	1	2	1	7
Plement, Thomas	0	0	0	1		2	0	0	1		11
Philips, Julius	0	0	0	0	1	0	0	0	1		
Pollard, John	0	0	1								
Parke, Edmund	0	1	1	0	1	0	0	1	0	1	12
Poindexter, Lightfoot	0	1	0	3		0	0	0	0	1	14
Pollard, Fielding	0	1	0	1		0	0	1			3
Porter, John	0	0	0	1		2	0	1			6
Perge, Jacob										4	
Porter, James	0	1	0	1		1	0	1	1	1	2
Parkinson, William	1	1	1	1		1	1	0	1	1	11
Philbabes, Edward	0	0	0	1		4	0	0	1		1
Patterson, Jesse										1	
Peerman, Thomas										9	
Parkison, Joseph	1	1	0	1		3	0	1		1	8
Parkison, Elizabeth						0	0	0	1		4
Pollard, Pleasant	1	3	0	1		1	0	1		1	4
Poindexter, Polley	0	2	0	1		2	0	2	1		11
Pollard, Robert	0	0	0	0	1	3	0	1			12
Pomfrey, William	1	0	0	1		2	0				3

Poor House	2	5	2	1		0	3	1	0	1	1	12
Pollard, Anne	0	1	0	0	1							2
Poindexter, Judith						0	0	1	1	1	1	2
Poindexter, Susan	0	1	0	0		1	0	2	1			7
Perkins, Robert	2	0	1	1		1	1	1	1			16
Pettey										5		
Pomfrey, Pleasant	0	0	0	1		1	0	0	2			3
Poindexter, S.John	0	1	1	1		0	1	1	0	1	1	21
Parish, John	2	1	0	1		2	0	0	1			14
Parish, William	1	1	0	1		1	1	0	1			
Quiggen, Susanna	1	1	1			1	0	0	2			9
Ragland, Dick										2		
Richardson, Edmund	1	0	2	1		1	0	0	1			7
Roberts, James	2	1	1	1		0	0	0	1			8
Ratcliffe, William	0	0	1			0	1					1
Redwood, John	0	0	1			0	2	0			1	5
Ratcliffe, Thomas	2	0	1	0	1	0	1	1	1		2	11
Richardson, William	0	0	1									3
Rainbow, Ned										5		
Ragland, George	0	0	0	1		3	0	1	0	1		13
Roper, William	0	0	2									1
Ross, Jane										2		
Russel, Armistead	0	0	0	1		2	0	2				45
Richardson, Holt	0	0	1	1								4
Richardson, Turner	2	1	0	1		4	1	0	1			6
Ross, William	1	1	1	1		2	1	0	1			
Russel, William	2	3	1	1		1	1	0	1			
Ratcliffe, William	0	0	0	0	1	0	1	0	0	1		4
Richardson, John	0	0	0	1		2	2	1				2
Roper, Eldridge	2	1	0	1		2	2	0	1	1		34
Robertson, Robert	1	0	2	0	1	0	0	0	1			7
Roper, John	0	1	1	0	1	1	0	5				3
Saunders, Isaac	0	0	0	0	1	0						10
Smith, Anne	1	2	1			0	0	1	0	1		14
Saunders, Julius	0	0	0	0	1	0	1	1	0	1		1
Sherman, Ballard	1	1	1	0	1	2	0	2	1			25
Smith, William	1	0	0	1		1	0	0	1			
Steward, John	0	0	1			2	0	1	0	1		1
Sweney, Elizabeth	0	1				0	0	0	1			
Steward, Lacy						1	0	0	1			
Steward, Thomas	3	1	0	1		1	1	0	1			16
Smithy, Polly	1	0	0	0		0	1	0	1			2
Smithy, Casander	0	0	0	1		0	1	0	0	1		
Spraggins, Mary										1		6
Stiff, Susanna	0	1				0	1	1	1			6
Sole, Sally									1			4
Saunders, George	0	0	0	1								
Slater, William	3	2	0	1		2	0	1	1			8
Slater, Mary	1	0	1			0	0	0	1	1		7
Slater, Daniel	0	0	0	1		1	0	1				4
Savage, Southy	2	0	0	1		0	0	1				19
Shell, Fanny	1	0				0	1	0	1			
Steward, Thomas S.	1	0	1			0	0	1				6
Sneed, Sally	0	1	0			0	1	0	1			4
Sweeney, Jonathan	1	1	0	1		2	1	0	1			1

Page 9

Page 10

Slater, Henly	1	0	0	0	1	0	0	0	1		2
Saunders, John	3	2	0	1		2	0	1	1		8
Sherman, Michael	1	0	0	0	1						30
Smith, John-	4	1	0	0	1	0	0	1	1		8
Smith, Charles	0	1	1	1	1	1	1	1	0	1	36
Tyree, Mary	1	1	0	0		0	1	1	1	1	8
Tallman, John	1	0	0	0	1	1	0	0	1		2
Twinney, John	0	0	1			0	0	1			
Terrel, William	1	1	0	0	1	0	2	0			4
Tayler, James	1	0	0	0	1	1	1	0	1		
Tyree, Elizabeth						0	0	2	0	1	
Turner, Charles	0	0	0	0	1	0	0	0	1		11
Tyree, William	0	1	2	0	1	0	0	1	2	1	2
Tyree, Francis	1	0	0	1		1	0	1	0	1	1	17
Tyree, Thomas	2	1	0	1		1	1	0	1		
Taylor, Sally	1	1	0			0	1	0	1		
Taylor, William	1	0	0	1		2	0	1	1		
Timberlake, Benj.	0	0	0	0	1	0	1	1			12
Timberlake, John	2	2	0	0	1	0	0	1	0	1	7
Tandy, John	2	0	0	1		3	1	0	1		6
Thomson, James	0	0	0	1		1	0	1	0	1	
Turner, Robert	1	0	0	1		2	1	0	1		3
Turner, Susanna	0	0	0	0	1	0	1	0			2
Thompson, John	2	1	0	0	1	0	0	2	1		
Tally, Fleming C.	0	0	3								6
Tyree, William	0	0	0	1		0	0	1	1		1
Tunstal, Thomas	1	0	0	1		0	1	0	1		16
Taylor, Clemens	1	0	0	1		4	0	1			21
Tandy, Elizabeth						2	0	1			6
Tyree, James	1	0	0	1		3	1	0	1		3
Thomson, Polly	0	0	0	1		0	0	0	0	1	
Tally, Nicholas	2	1	0	1		0	0	0	1		
Tyree, Batts	0	0	1								
Tyree, Dickey	0	0	0	0	1	0	0	0	0	2	4
Tyree, Henry	0	0	0	1							
Tyree, Richard	0	0	0	1		2	0	1			8
Taylor, Wm.R.	0	0	2			0	0	0	0	2	10
Taylor, Mary	0	1	2			0	0	1	0	1	1
Taylor, Richardson	0	0	0	1		1	0	0	1		2
Timberlake, Richard	1	0	0	1		1	0	0	1		10
Taylor, Talsey	1	0	0	0		1	0	0	1		
Tucker, Miles	1	0	0	1		1	0	0	1		
Taylor, William	3	3	0	1		1	0	0	1	5	3
Trower, Lucy	1	0	1	0		0	0	0	2	1	3
Vaiden, Jeremiah	1	2	0	0	1	2	1	0	1		18
Vaiden, Isaac	3	1	0	0	1	1	0	0	1		22
Valentine, Joseph	0	0	1			2	0	1			5
Vaughan, Marie A											6
Vaughan, Pryor						0	0	1			2
Vaiden, Henry	0	0	1			0	0	1	0	1	1	13
Vaiden, Thomas	1	0	0	1		0	0	1			11
Vaughan, Henry	2	0	1			1	2	0	1		5
Vaiden, Elizabeth Jr.	1	0	1	1		0	0	0	1		7
Vaiden, Elizabeth	0	0	2			0	0	1	0	1	6
Vaiden, Micajah	1	0	0	1		0	2	1	1		7

Willis, William	1	0	0	1		3	0	1	1	0	1	9
Walker, Florence	3	2	0	1		0	0	0	1			
Williams, James	3	4	2	0	1	0	1	2	2	1		29
Woodward, Bartlet	0	0	1			0						6
Wilkins, John	2	0	0	1		0	1					
Walker, David	3	1	2	1		1	3	1	1			1
Wyatt, John	0	0	1	0	1	1	1	1	1			11
Wilkes, Reuben	0	0	0	1		2	0	1				3
Wilkes, John	0	0	1	0	1	1	1	1	1			11
Waddil, Elizabeth	0	1				2	0	0	1			1
Whitcomb, Rebecca	0	0	0	0	1	0	0	0	0	1		
Web, George											1	2
Walls, Elizabeth	1	0	1			0	0	1	0	1		
Watkins, John D.	1	0	0	1		1	1	1	2			37
Wilkinson, Susanna	1	0	0	0		1	1	0	1			30
Wade, David	2	0	0	1		0	1	0	1			3
Winfrey, Major	0	0	0	0	1					1		6
Woodward, Richmond	1	0	0	0		0	0	0	1			
Wilkins, James	0	0	1			0	0	1	1			6
Warren, John	0	1										
Wade, Pleasant	0	0	2			0	0	0	0	1		
Warner, John	1	0	0	1		2	1	0	1			
Williams, David												7
Wright, Judith	0	1	0	0	0	3	1	1	2			1
Williams, Bartlet	0	1	0	0	1	0	0	0	1			9
Wilkinson, James P.	0	0	1	1		0	1	4				4
Winfrey, Austin	2	0	0	0	1	1	1	1	1			8
Walls, Richard	1	0	0	1		0	0	0	1			
Woodward, Warwick	1	0	0	1		0	0	2				1
Williams, Meredith	1	1	0	1		2	1	0	1			5
Williams, Dudley	0	0	1			0	0	1				3
Walls, Thomas	0	0	1			0	0	0	1			
Williams, William H	1	0	0	1		2	0	0	1			8
Waddel, Mary	0	0	1	1		1	0	0	0	1		20
Winfrey, William	2	1	2	0		1	0	0	1			
White, Nathaniel	3	0	0	1		2	0	0	1			2
Wade, Martin	1	0	0	1		1	0	0	1			1
Webb, John S.	1	0	0	1		0	1	0				8
Wright, Henry	2	2	1	1		0	0	1	0	1		3
Woodram, John	2	0	1			0	0	1	0	1		
Wade, Gideon	1	0	0	1		0	0	1				
Wright, Richard	0	1	0	1	1	1	0	3	0	1		
Webb, Lewis	3	2	0	0	1	1	0	1	1			3
Woodward, Martha	0	0				0	2	3	0	1		
Wilkinson, Sarah	0					0	1	1	0	1		13
Wilkinson, George (Lawyer)	0	0	0	1								1
Webb, Conrad	1	0	2	1		0	0	1				40
Woodward, Henry	2	0	0	1		0	0	0	1			3
Wilkinson, James	0	0	0	1		0	0	0	0	1		14
Woodward, Joseph	0	0	2	0	1	0	0	1			1	13
Young, William H.	0	0	1			0	0	1				
Yates, Richard	1	0	0	1		2	0	0	1			3
Young, James	1	2	0	0	1	1	0	0	1			11

1220 males, 1225 females, 308 free negroes, 3725 slaves: total 6,478.

SEVENTH U. S. CENSUS

1850.

NEW KENT COUNTY, VIRGINIA.

Taken on the 2nd. to 27th. days of August, 1850, by

Bat. D. Christian, Ass't Marshall.

(Only white inhabitants are included

in this copy. There were

............blacks

in the county.)

No. of Family	Name	Age	Sex	Occupation	Value of Real Estate	Birth place	Married within the Yr.	Over 20 & Illiterate
1	Gideon Wade	69	M	Farming	1,200	Va.		1
	Polley Broughton	45	F			Va.		1
2	Sarah Macon	75	F		23,360	Va.		
	Mary S. Nelson	35	F		1,000	Va.		
	Edw. P. Chamberlayne	29	M	Farming		Va.		D&D
	Julia A. Batkim	20	F			Va.		
	Thomas M. Page	20	M	None		Va.		
	Lucy A. Govan or Goran	34	F			Va.		
	James Govan	8	M			Va.		
3	Joseph Minor	45	M	Overseer		Va.		
	Ann Minor	34	F			Va.		
	George, C. Minor	8	M			Va.		
	Thomas H. Minor	4	M			Va.		
	Henry C. Minor	1	M			Va.		
4	George T. Burmley	26	M	Farming	12,000	Va.		
	Ann B. Johnson	40	F			Va.		
	Maria E. Johnson	13	F			Va.		
	Lucy Ann Johnson	12	F			Va.		
5	Wm. C. Madison	29	M	Farming		Va.	1	
	Lucy A. Madison	17	F			Va.	1	
6	Robert Martin	37	M	Hunting fishing		Va.		
	Elvira Martin	34	F			Va.		
	Philany A. Martin	17	F			Va.		
	Major Martin	15	M			Va.		
	Wm. A. Martin	9	M			Va.		
	Angelina Martin	6	F			Va.		
	Isabella Martin	3	F			Va.		
7	Isaac Tyree	67	M	Farming	1,200	Va.		
8	William Dozier	33	M	Lumberman		Va.		
9	Henry Webb	58	M		25,600	Va.		
	Mary A. Webb	55	F			Va.		
	John Huxstep	18	M	None		Va.		
10	Thomas French	50	M	Farming		Va.		
	Lucretia French	39	F			Va.		
	Polley, D. French	13	F			Va.		
	Frances E. French	11	F			Va.		
	Portia French	9	F			Va.		
	Thomas I. French	7	M			Va.		
	Martha A. C. French	4	F			Va.		
11.	John B. Patterson	32	M	Farming		Va.		
	Mary I. Patterson	25	F			Va.		
	Jno. T. Patterson	3	M			Va.		
	Alice C. Patterson	6/12	F			Va.		
12	George W. Robineau	30	M	Farming	1,200	Va.		
	Geo. W. Robineau. Sr	60	M	Doctor		Va.		
	Mary F. Robineau	50	F			Va.		
	Maria Robineau	20	F			Va.		

No. of Family	Name	Age	Sex	Occupation	Value of Real Estate	Birth Place	Married within the Yr.	Over 20 & Illiterate
13	Havilah Ellyson	44	M	Farming	$2,000	Va.		
	Elizabeth Ellyson	45	F			Va.		
	Betty F. Ellyson	20	F			Va.		
	Lemuel G. Ellyson	17	M			Va.		
	Nancy A. Ellyson	14	F			Va.		
	Havilah T. Ellyson	11	M			Va.		
	William P. Ellyson	8	M			Va.		
14	Frances A. Tunstall	54	F		1,500	Va.		
	Thomas C. Tunstall	29	M	Farming	240	Va.		
	William R. Tunstall	24	M	Farming	1,000	Va.		
15	John P. Boyd	52	M	Farming	5,000	Va.		
	Sally B. Boyd	40	F			Va.		
	Martha W. Godwin	45	F			Va.		
	George G. Boyd	22	M	None		Va.		
	William R. Boyd	15	M			Va.		
	Martha I. Boyd	7	F			Va.		
	Alwilda C. Boyd	4	F			Va.		
	Earl Boyd	4/12	M			Va.		
16	Samuel C. Anderson	38	M	Farming		Va.		
	Sarah Mason	54	F			Va.		
	Eliz. A. Anderson	22	F			Va.		
	James Anderson	11	M			Va.		
	Ellen Anderson	5	F			Va.		
	Sarah Anderson	1	F			Va.		
17	Wm. H. Vaiden, Sr	50	M.	Farming	684	Va.		
	Susan V. Vaiden	48	F			Va.		
	Georgianna Wade	17	F			Va.		
	Sarah M. Vaiden	17	F			Va.		
	Susan I. Wade	14	F			Va.		
	Fluvanna S. Vaiden	13	F			Va.		
	Mary Jane Vaiden	8	F			Va.		
18	Ro. A. Hill	35	M.	Farming	3,600	Va.		
	Martha A. Hill	32	F			Va.		
	Juliet I. Hill	13	F			Va.		
	Harriett, C. Hill	12	F			Va.		
	Martha I. Hill	8	F			Va.		
	Augustine Hill	4	M			Va.		
	Almira Hill	2	F			Va.		
19	Braxton Garlick	39	M	Farming	50,000	Va.		
	Mary C Garlick	32	F			Va.		
	Henrietta Garlick	14	F			Va.		
	James H. Garlick	7	M			Va.		
	Medora B. Garlick	4/12	F			Va.		
20	Henry Smith	50	M	Minister		N.S.P. Va.		
	Eliza B. Smith	33	F			Va.		
	Henry L. Smith	9	M			Va.		
	Martha B. Smith	7	F			Va.		
	Mitchell Adams	29	M	Farming		Va.		
	Ann Adams	26	F			Va.		
	Watkins Adams	3	M			Va.		

No. of Family	Name	Age	Sex	Occu-pation	Value of Real Estate	Birth Place	Married within the Yr.	Over 20 & illiterate.
21	Fielding H. Crump	24	M	Farming	$1,200	Va.		
	William C. Wade	22	M	Farming		Va.		
22	Richard Phillips	30	M	Farming	500	Va.		
	Elizabeth Phillips	20	F			Va.		
	James W. Phillips	2	M			Va.		
	Jane Phillips	3/12	F			Va.		
	Lucy Gethright	20	F			Va.		1
	Joe Slaughter	16	M	Farming		Va.		
	Joshua Wicker	16	M	Farming		Va.		
23	Edw. P. Meredith	34	M	Farming	4,000	Va.		
	John H. Vaiden	20	M	Farming		Va.		
	Robert Meredith	9	M			Va.		
	Henry Meredith	7	M			Va.		
	Jos. T. Meredith	5	M			Va.		
	Selina P. Meredith	4	F			Va.		
24	Bailey Barker	51	M	Farming	441	Va.		
	Martha Barker	51	F			Va.		1
	Octavia Barker	14	F			Va.		
25	Henry Barker	36	M	Farming	50	Va.		1
	H. D. Clopton	38	M	Farming		Va.		
26	Richard Wright	24	M	Farming		Va.		1
27	Emiley Meredith	53	F			Va.		
	Ann E. Meredith	26	F			Va.		
	Mary Meredith	20	F			Va.		
	Winston Meredith	17	M	None		Va.		
	Thos. Meredith	13	M			Va.		
	Emiley Meredith	13	F			Va.		
	Wm A. Meredith	12	M			Va.		
28	Wm. Anderson	29	M	Farming	2,500	Va.		
	Matilda A. Anderson	28	F			Va.		
	John H. Anderson	7	M			Va.		
	Emuella Anderson	5	F			Va.		
	Willianna Anderson	1	F			Va.		
29	Emiley Batkins	33	F		1,500	Va.		
	Mary Ann Batkins	16	F			Va.		
	Martha A. Higgins	33	F			Va.		1
	Harriet E. Batkins	13	F			Va.		
	Benj. M. Batkins	11	M			Va.		
	Geo. W. Batkins	9	M			Va.		
	Lucy B. Batkins	5	F			Va.		
30	Edwin I. Clopton	80	M	Farming	4,000	Va.		
	Edwin I. Clopton, Jr	20	M	Farming		Va.		
	Maria Clopton	23	F			Va.		
	Mary E. C. Clopton	6/12	F			Va.		
31	Samuel Webb	54	M	Farming	20,000	Va.		
	Freeman G. Clarke	34	M	Farming	400	Va.		
32	Geo. S. Merriman	37	M	Farming		Va.		1
	Jane Merriman	27	F			Va.		1
	Frances E. Merriman	11	F			Va.		
	Martha I. Merriman	8	F			Va.		
	Sarah A. Merriman	6	F			Va.		

No. of Family	Name	Age	Sex	Occupation	Value of Real Estate	Birth Place	Married within the Yr.	Over 20 & illiterate
32	William T. Merriman	3	M			Va.		
	Richard G. Merriman	6/12	M			Va.		
33	Cath: Mason	37	F			Va.		1
	Thos. B. Mason	22	M	None		Va.		1
	Ro: M. Mason	20	M	None		Va.		1
34	Sarah Ellett	40	F			Va.		
	Cornelius Ellett	19	M	None		Va.		
	Lucy Ann M. Ellett	16	F			Va.		
	Beverley Ellett	13	M			Va.		
	William T. Ellett	9	M			Va.		
	Sarah Ellett	7	F			Va.		
	James Houchings	26	M	Farming		Va.		1
35	Miles C. Tunstall	43	M	Farming	$3,000	Va.		
	Eliza Tunstall	35	F			Va.		
	Lucy T. Burton	27	F			Va.		
	Martha C. Tunstall	18	F			Va.		
	Thos. R. Tunstall	17	M	none		Va.		
	Miles C. Tunstall	15	M			Va.		
	Peter C. Foster	13	M			Va.		
	Ann E. Tunstall	12	F			Va.		
	Alice Tunstall	3	F			Va.		
36	Charles Pearson	62	M	Farming	4,000-	Va.		
	Elizabeth Pearson	62	F			Va.		
	Sarah Pearson	30	F			Va.		
	Betty Pearson	25	F			Va.		
	Mary Pearson	20	F			Va.		
	Robinnett Pearson	16	F			Va.		
	Frances D. Bailey	70	F			Va.		
38	Clarissa Grant	63	F		2,000	Va.		
	James C. Grant	25	M	Farming		Va.		
	Cath; Grant	21	F			Va.		
39	Josiah Higgins Sr.	65	M	Farming	1,000	Va.		
	Josiah Higgins, Jr.	28	M	Farming	60	Va.		
	Eliz. H. Higgins	63	F			Va.		
	Ann E. Higgins	43	F			Va.		
41	Theo. H. Woodward	38	M	Tailor	1,000	Va.		
	Mary A. Woodward	32	F			Va.		
	Mary A. Woodward	7	F			Va.		
	Augustus Woodward	1	M			Va.		
42	William G. Nero	56	M	Carpenter	400	Va.		
	Naomi Nero	58	F			Va.		
	Frances Nero	21	F			Va.		
	Virginia Nero	18	F.			Va.		
43	Geo. B. P. Borvis or Bowis?	50	M	Farming	800	Va.		
	Julia A. Borvis	48	F			Va.		
	Sally P. Borvis	22	F			Va.		
	Mary I. Borvis	20	F			Va.		
	Barbara Anna Borvis	17	F			Va.		
	Betty Borvis	12	F			Va.		
	Georgella Borvis	8	F			Va.		
	Edward A. Borvis	5	M			Va.		

No. of Family	Name	Age	Sex	Occupation	Value of Real Estate	Birth Place	Married within the Yr.	Over 20 & illiterate
46	C.A. Hewlett	50	M	Farming	$1,000	Va.		
	Matilda B. Hewlett	17	F			Va.		
	Maria L. Lewlett	16	F			Va.		
	Mary F. Hewlett	14	F			Va.		
47	Wm. H. Roper	37	M	Farming	600	Va.		
	Louisa M. Roper	37	F			Va.		
	James B. Hopkins	50	M	Carpenter		Va.		
	Ro: R. Roper	22	M	Carpenter		Va.		
48	Fleming T. Crump	48	M	Farming	4,200	Va.		
	Martha E. Crump	21	F			Va.		
	Sarah E. Crump	9/12	F			Va.		
	Betsey Hix	41	F			Va		1
49	Wm. L. Wilkinson	48	M	Farming	350	Va.		
	Roseann Wilkinson	40	F			Va.		
	Thomas Wilkinson	12	M			Va.		
	Wm. C. Wilkinson	9	M			Va.		
	Roseann Wilkinson	6	F			Va.		
	Willinette Wilkinson	6	F			Va.		
	Leonidas A. Wilkinson	5	M			Va.		
50	Edmond W. Allen	30	M	Farming	1,200	Va.		
	Eliza D. Allen	28	F			Va.		
	John W. Allen	7	M			Va.		
	Sarah A. Allen	7	F			Va.		
	Paulina I. Allen	5	F			Va.		
	Lucy D. Allen	4	F			Va.		
	Tho. W. Allen	2	M			Va.		
	Edmond H. Allen	1	M			Va.		
	Joseph Wade	18	M	none		Va.		
	David Tyler	12	M			Va.		
51	Ro. S. Pollard	37	M	Farming	800	Va.		
	Sarah M. Pollard	25	F			Va.		
	Alice C. Pollard	7	F			Va.		
	John S. Pollard	5	M			Va.		
	Ro. I. Pollard	3	M			Va.		
52	John T. Hill	48	M	Carpenter	1,950	Va.		
	Tabitha Hill	48	F			Va.		
	Josephine T. Hill	12	F			Va.		
	Richard A. Hill	8	M			Va.		
53	James T. Sherman	44	M	Farming	1,895	Va.		
	Ann C. Sherman	51	F			Va.		
54	Nancy Sherman	75	F			Va.		
55	Richard Hockaday	30	M	Farming	400	Va.		
	Elizabeth Hockaday	58	F			Va.		
	Martha Hockaday	32	F			Va.		
	Philmer Hockaday	13	M			Va.		
	Elizabeth Hockaday	4/12	F			Va.		
56	John Parrish	45	M	Farming	1,500	Va.		
	Minerva D. Parrish	30	F			Va.		
	William F. Parrish	18	M	Teacher		Va.		

No. of Family	Name	Age	Sex	Occupation	Value of Real Estate	Birthplace	Married within the Yr.	Over 20 & illiterate
	Amanda S. Parrish	16	F			Va.		
	Marcus A. Parrish	9	M			Va.		
	Mary E. Parrish	12	F			Va.		
	Ann E. Parrish	7	F			Va.		
	John B. Parrish	4	M			Va.		
	Geo. I. Parrish	3	M			Va.		
59	John B. Vaiden	28	M	Farming	$300	Va.		1
	Judith T. Vaiden	25	F			Va.		
	Rebecca Vaiden	50	F			Va.		
	Edmond T. Jones	60	M	Painter		Va.		
60	Wm Acree	40	M	Farming	700	Va.		
	James Hughes	19	M	Farming		Va.		
61	John Acree	57	M	Farming	800	Va.		
	Eliza Acree	53	F			Va.		
62	Wm. F. Trimmier	31	M	Carpenter		Va.		
	Mary Trimmier	32	F			Va.		
	James H. Trimmier	6	M			Va.		
	Thos. L. Trimmier	3	M			Va.		
63	Wm. H. Courtney	50	M	Farming	750	Va.		
	Martha A. Courtney	39	F			Va.		
	Wm. H. Courtney, Jr	19	M	Farming		Va.		
	Benj. Courtney	15	M			Va.		
	Robert Courtney	14	M			Va.		
	Mary Courtney	9	F			Va.		
	Naomi Courtney	7	F			Va.		
	Selina Courtney	4	F			Va.		
65	Mary Dobson	55	F		2,000	Va.		
	John Dobson	28	M	Farming		Va.		
	Ro: P. Jerdone	24	M	none		Va.		
	James D. Crump	2	M			Va.		
	Roseanna D. Earnest	15	F			Va.		
66	Martha Barker	58	F			Va.		1
	Edney B. Barker	25	F			Va.		1
	Dolly Barker	40	F			Va.		1
67	Joseph Johnson	40	F			Va.		1
	Polley Johnson	35	F			Va		1
	John Johnson	14	M			Va.		
	Joseph Johnson	11	M			Va		
	Wilson Burnett	45	M			Va.		
68	Ferdinand Bacon	37	M	Farming	75	Va.	1	1
	Harriet Bacon	21	F			Va	1	
	William E. Bacon	6	M			Va.		
69	Dabney Wade	30	M	Farming	800	Va.		1
	Martha Wade	60	F			Va.		1
	Dica Wade	23	F			Va.		1
	Martha Wade	50	F			Va.		
70.	William B. Goode	32	M	Farming	1,350	Va.		
	Lucy F. Goode	26	F			Va.		
	Bat; Hill	30	M	none		Va.		1
	Alena F. Goode	3	F			Va.		
	Wm. Goode, Jr.	1	M			Va.		

No. of Family	Name	Age	Sex	Occu-pation	Value of Real Estate	Birth Place	Married within the Yr.	Over 20 & illit-erate.
71	Wesley P. Bennett	25	M	Farming	$1,500	Va.		
	Margaret K. Bennett	23	F			Va.		
	Charles W. Bennett	3	M			Va.		
72	Jos. H. Goode	24	M	Farming	900	Va.		
	Cath. C. Goode	60	F			Va.		1
	Robert Goode	28	M	Farming		Va.		1
73	Joseph Wicker	25	M	none		Va.		1
	John Wicker	24	M	none		Va.		1
	William Wicker	20	M	none		Va.		1
	Martha Wicker	18	F			Va.		
74.	William E. Martin	55	M	Farming		Va.		
	Mary E. Martin	40	F			Va.		
	Mary E. Martin	18	F			Va.		
	Ro. S. Martin	15	M	none		Va.		
	Cordelia Martin	4	F			Va.		
	Martha A. W. Martin	2	F			Va.		
75	Martin Wade	76	M	Farming	185	Va.		
	Ann Wade	31	F			Va.		1
	David Wade	27	M	none		Va.		1
	Bentley Wicker	14	M			Va.		
76	Ro. T. Turner	46	M	Farming		Va.		
	Mary E. Turner	19	F			Va.		
	Ro. E. Turner	15	F			Va.		
	Susan V. Turner	12	F			Va.		
	Octavia A. Turner	9	F			Va.		
	Emily F. Turner	6	F			Va.		
77.	Ro. T. Turner	77	M	Farming	700	Va.		
	Cath. Turner	56	F			Va.		1
	Eliz. A. Terrell	43	F			Va.		1
	William Turner	33	M	Farming		Va.		
	Allen A. Terrell	20	M	none		Va.		1
	Eliz. A. Terrell	17	F.			Va.		
	Joseph C. Terrell	14	M			Va.		
	Casandra Terrell	12	F			Va.		
	Littleberry Terrell	10	M			Va.		
	Lurena Terrell	8	F			Va.		
	Delia A. Terrell	4	F			Va.		
	Ara. A. Terrell	8/12	F			Va.		
78	William R. Savage	40	M	Doctor	2,400	Va.		
	Ann S. Savage	29	F			Va.		
	Aaron Fussil	23	M	Farming		Va.		
	William W. Savage	16	M			Va.		
79	Matthew H. Burnett	41	M	Farming	350	Va.		
	Lucy A. Burnett	34	F			Va		1
	Frances E. Burnett	10	F			Va.		
	Jno H. Burnett	8	M			Vs.		
	William D. Burnett	5	M			Va.		
	Lucy A. A. Burnett	2	F			Va.		
	Matthew W. Burnett	9.12	M			Va.		

No. of Family	Name	Age	Sex	Occupation	Value of Real Estate	Birth Place	Married within the Yr.	Over 20 & illiterate
80	James Chadick	54	M	Farming		Va.		
	Martha A. Chadick	57	F			Va.		
	Eliza Martin	80	F			Va.		
	Sarah A. Chadick	31	F			Va		1 Bl
	Mary L. Chadick	29	F			Va.		1 Bl
	Martha A. Chadick	22	F			Va.		
	Cath. E. Chadick	20	F			Va.		
	Jno. I. Chadick	18	M	None		Va.		
81	Poindexter Higgins	34	M	Farming	$ 200	Va.		
	Elizabeth Higgins	32	F			Va.	1	
	Mary Burnett	40	F			Va.	1	
	Mary L. Higgins	8	F			Va.		
	Pat. H. Higgins	4	M			Va.		
	James H. Kelley	8	M			Va.		
82	Richard A. Tucker	61	M	Shoemaker		Va.		
	Elizabeth Tucker	62	F			Va.		
	George Tucker	50	M	none		Va.	1	
82	Elicabeth Martin	42	F			Va.		
	Betsey Terrell	18	F			Va.		
	R. M. Martin	8	M			Va.		
	James H. Martin	5	M			Va.		Bl
	Eliz. C. Martin	4	F			Va.		
84	Ro. C. Terrell	55	M	Farming	200	Va.	1	
	Frances A. Terrell	50	F			Va.		
	Frances A. Terrell	20	F			Va.		
	Parthena Terrell	18	F			Va.		
	Virginia Terrell	16	F			Val		
	Cornelia Terrell	13	F			Va.		
	Martha Terrell	8	F			Va.		
85	John Adams	41	M	Wheelright	400	Va.		
	Mary Adams	49	F			Va.		
	Ferdinand D. Martin	27	M	none		Va	1	
	John Adams	17	M	none		Va		
	Ann S. Adams	17	F			Va.		
	Ro. E. Adams	14	M			Va.		
	William Adams	11	M			Va.		
	Richard Adams	9	M			Va.		
	Dematins Adams	4	M			Va.		
86	Eliza Higgins	45	F			Va.		1
	Jernn Higgins	24	F			Va.		1
	John Higgins	16	M	none		Va.		
87	Patsey Martin	56	F			Va.		1
	Parke, F. Martin	12	M			Va.		
	Patsey Chappel	30	F			Va.		1
	Henry Chappel	10	M			Va.		
	Eliz. Chappel	13	F			Va.		
88	Thos Martin	39	M	Farming	550	Va.		
	Harriet Martin	29	F			Va.		
	Virginia Martin	2	F			Va.		
	Thomas Martin	11/12	M			Va.		

No. of Family	Name	Age	Sex	Occupation	Value of Real Estate	Birth Place	Married within the Yr.	Over 20 & illiterate
89	Joseph I. Peace	28	M	Farming	$450	Va.		
	Roselin Peace	23	F			Va.		
	Alonzo Peace	4	M			Va.		
	Julia Peace	3	F			Va.		
90	Jos. F. McGhee	30	M	Farming	1,200	Va.	1	
	Elmira McGhee	18	F			Va.	1	
91	Benjamin Goodman	53	M	Farming	200	Va.		1
	Agnes A. Goodman	40	F			Va.		1
	Sarah A. Baker	22	F			Va.		1
	Benj. E. Goodman	15	M	none		Va.		
	Charles H. Goodman	14	M			Va.		
	Leroy D. Goodman	11	M			Va.		
	Maria A. Goodman	9	F			Va.		
	Wm. H. Goodman	7	M			Va.		
	Jas. E. Goodman	5	M			Va.		
	Louisa V. Goodman	2	F			Va.		
92	John Barker	30	M	Farming		Va.		1
	Reuben Hughes	75	M	none		Va.		1
	William Barker	22	M	none		Va.		1
93	Nathan L. Savage	43	M	Farming	9,500	Va.		
	Eliz. A. Savage	40	F			Va.		
	Southey L. Savage	18	M	Dep. Sheriff		Va.		
	William A. F. Savage	15	M			Va.		
	Norton R. Savage	13	M			Va.		
	Sarah F. Savage	12	F			Va.		
	Mary E. Savage	5	F			Va.		
	Maria P. Savage	3	F			Va.		
	Philn. P. Frayser	18	M	none		Va.		
	Elvira C. Frayser	13	F			Va.		
94	Mary Clopton	40	F			Va.		
	Mary I. Clopton	9	F			Va.		
95	John Higgins	30	M	none		Va.		
96	Elizabeth Higgins	50	F		400	Va.		1
	Jos. F. Higgins	21	M	none		Va.		
	Saml. D. Higgins	14	M			Va.		
	Matthew A. Higgins	11	M			Va.		
	Fanny Daniel	50	F			Va.		1
97	Thos. D. Chadick	47	M	Farming	700	Va.		
	Sarah A. Chadick	40	F			Va.		
	Wm. T. Chadick	17	M	none		Va.		
	Sarah E. Chadick	8	F			Va.		
99	William Terrell	50	M	Farming	1,000	Va.		
	Ro. C. Terrell	20	M	none		Va.		1
	William Terrell	18	M	none		Va.		
	Henry C. Terrell	15	M	none		Va.		
	Thos. H. Terrell	13	M			Va.		
	Martin D. Terrell	9	M			Va.		
	Geo. A. Terrell	7	M			Va.		
	Wash. F. Terrell	5	M			Va.		
	Ann E. Terrell	13	F			Va.		
	Mary R. Terrell	2	F			Va.		

Page 22

No. of Family	Name	Age	Sex	Occupation	Value of Real Estate	Birth Place	Married within the Yr.	Over 20 & illiterate
	Caroline A. Terrell	42	F			Va.		1
	Benj. A. Thomas	22	M	none		Va.		
100.	Joshua Higgins	45	M	none	$150	Va.		1
	Mary Higgins	35	F			Va.		1
	Rosalin Higgins	16	F			Va.		
	Nancy Higgins	14	F			Va.		
	Miles Higgins	10	M			Va.		
	William Higgins	7	M			Va.		
	Catharine Higgins	1	F			Va.		
101	Rebecca Ellyson	51	F			Va.		1
	Emeline Ellyson	26	F			Va.		
	Helen Ellyson	24	F			Va.		
	Henrietta Ellyson	19	F			Va.		
	Richard Ellyson	11	M			Va.		
	Alice Ellyson	5	F			Va.		
102	Daniel Ellyson	50	M	Farming	1,000	Va.		
	Martha Ellyson	45	F			Va.		
	Collier H. Ellyson	21	M	none		Va.		
	Mary D. Ellyson	16	F			Va.		
	Louisa Ellyson	24	F			Va.		
	Ellen Ellyson	6	F			Va.		
	Saml. Ellyson	5	M			Va.		
103	James Ellyson	59	M	Farming		Va.		
	Marjery Ellyson	80	F			Va.		
	Julia Ellyson	64	F			Va.		
	Julia A. Ellyson	26	F			Va.		
	Alfred B. Ellyson	24	M	none		Va.		
104	Mary Moss	85	F			Va.		
105	Thos. Wright	52	M.	Farming	150	Va.		
	Martha Wright (Martha A.)	24	F			Va.		
	Mary Wright	22	F			Va.		
	Henry T. Wright	21	M	none		Va.		
	Wm. Jos. Wright	15	M	none		Va.		
	Pleasant Wright	12	M			Va.		
	Jno. A. Wright	10	M			Va.		
	Eliz. Wright	8	F			Va.		
106	Harriet Savage	66	F		1,000	Va.		
	Geo. Hankins	5	M			Va.		
107	Saml. M. Moody	47	M	Farming	1,200	Va.		
	Harriet W. Moody	32	F			Va.		
	Martha Moody	80	F			Va.		
	Mary W. Moody	44	F			Va.		
	Eliz. D. Moody	38	F			Va.		
	Maria A. Moody	35	F			Va.		
	Jos. White	17	M	none		Va.		
	Thos. I. Moody	5	M			Va.		
	Sarah I. Moody	3	F			Va.		
	Martha A. Moody	1	F			Va.		
108	Jno. T. Fussell	56	M	Farming		Va.		
	Frances W. Fussell	20	F			Va.		1
	Mary Fussell	55	F			Va.		1
	Mary I. Fussell	15	F.			Va.		

No. of Family	Name	Age	Sex	Occupation	Value of Real Estate	Birth Place	Married within the Yr.	Over 20 & illiterate
109	Susan B. Royster	47	F			Va.		
	Betsey Kunningham?	40	F			Va.		
	Patsey Terrey	30	F			Va.		
	Elizabeth Royster	17	F			Va.		
	Harriett Royster	16	F			Va.		
	Ellen Royster	13	F			Va.		
	Lawrence Royster	9	M			Va.		
110	Wm. A. Dandridge	39	M	Farming	$1,600	Va.		
	Willinette R. Dandridge	22	F.			Va.		
	Bat. Dandridge	4	M			Va.		
	Eliz. W. Dandridge	1	F			Va.		
111	Richmond H. Terrell	24	M	Carpenter	400	Va.		
114	Reuben Moss	66	M	Farming	1,100	Va.		
	Susan B. Moss	41	F			Va.		
	Susan W. Moss	16	F			Va.		
	Ro. I. Moss	14	M			Va.		
	Betty F. Moss	6	F			Va.		
	Harriett M. Moss	5	F			Va.		
	Reubenette Moss	4	F			Va.		
115	Edmond W. Howle	45	M	Farming	400	Va.		
	Mary Howle	35	F			Va.		1
	Susan F. Howle	12	F			Va.		
	Ann V. Howle	9	F			Va.		
116	Martha P. Brims?(Binns)	38	F			Va.		1
	John Binns	13	M			Va.		
	William E. Binns	12	M			Va.		
117	Harriet P. Ratcliffe	42	F		1,500	Va.		
	Wm. F. Terrell	21	M	Teacher		Va.		
	Eliz. B. Marston	64	F			Va.		
Tavern	Cornelia Ratcliffe	17	F			Va.		
	Geo. T. Ratcliffe	15	M			Va.		
	Olivia E. Ratcliffe	13	F			Va.		
	Benj. H. Ratcliffe	11	M			Va.		
	John Ratcliffe	9	M			Va.		
118	Ann Eppes	41	F		3,000	Va.		
	John T. Eppes	19	M	Farming		Va.		
	Jane E. Eppes	17	F			Va.		
	Sally A. Eppes	13	F			Va.		
	Edward Eppes	11	M			Va.		
119	John Tucker Agt.	31	M	Farming	7,500	Va.		
120	Lucy M. Smithie	42	F		2,500	Va.		
	George Smithie	21	M	Farming		Va.		
	Ro. F. Carter	26	M	Farming		Va.	1	
	Eliz. B. Carter	19	F			Va.	1	
	Wm. M. Smithie	16	M	None		Va.		
	Pleasant T. Smithie	14	M			Va.		
121	Wm I. Morgan	49	M	Farming	4,800	Va.		
	Jane P Morgan	32	F			Va.		
	Ann M. Taylor	59	F			Va.		

No of Family	Name	Age	Sex	Occupation	Value of Real Estate	Birth Place	Married within the Yr.	Over 20 & illiterate
	Lucenia N. Morgan	5	F			Va.		
	Wm. P. Morgan	4	M			Va.		
	Edward T. Morgan	2	M			Va.		
	Laura I. Morgan	7/12	F			Va.		
122	Ann M. Fisher	40	F		$2,000	Va.		
	Patsey Capada	50	F			Va.		
	Geo. W. Fisher	14	M			Va.		
123	Anderson Crump	75	M	Farming	2,500	Va.		
	Debora Pond	60	F			Va.		
124	Wm A. Crump	26	M	Farming	500	Va.		
	Mary I. Crump	20	F			Va.		
125	Richard Crump	62	M	Farming	10,000	Va.		
	Matilda H. Crump	45	F			Va.		
	Ro. D. Crump	34	M	Farming		Va.		
	John Crump	32	M	Painter		Va.		
	Richard Crump	26	M	none		Va.		
	Columbus Crump	25	M	Carpenter		Va.	1	
	C. I. Crump	17	F			Va.	1	
	Mary C. Crump	17	F			Va.		
	Jno. Lewis P. Crump	15	M	none		Va.		
	Josephine Crump	11	F			Va.		
	Henry C. Crump	8	M			Va.		
	Zac. T. Crump	3	M			Va.		
126	Cornelius S. Crump	25	M	Farming	5,000	Va.		
	Mary B. Crump	25	F			Va.		
	Geo. P. Crump	22	M	Farming		Va.		
	Camilla S. Crump	27	F			Va.		
	Rebecca Frayser	19	F			Va.		
	Benj. D. Gary	26	M	none		Va.		
	Spencer C. Crump	3	M			Va.		
	Mary J. Crump	5/12	F			Va.		
127	Chr. M. Crump	53	M	Farming	1,000	Va.		
	Susan E. B Crump	42	F			Va.		
	Sarah A. Gary	27	F			Va.		
	Marietta Gary	4	F			Va.		
	Willinette Gary	2	F			Va.		
	Gary	1/12	M			Va.		
128	Sarah Bradley	68	F		1,000	Va.		
	Matthew Gary	31	M	none		Va.		1
129	James F. Parkinson	36	M	Farming	2,000	Va.		
	Ellen A. Parkinson	64	F			Va.		
	Hannah D. Parkinson	27	F			Va.		
	Jos. W. Parkinson	8	M			Va.		
	C. D. Parkinson	6	F			Va.		
	Mary E. Parkinson	4	F			Va.		
	Wm. A. Parkinson	1	M			Va.		
	George Hill	19	M	none		Va.		

No of Family	Name	Age	Sex	Occupation	Value of Real Estate	Birth Place	Married within the Yr.	Over 20 & illiterate
130	Ben. McKenzie	50	M	Farming	$2,000	Va.		
	Coley Austin	36	F			Va.		
	Martha Chandler	27	F			Va.		
	Susan A. B. McKenzie	21	F			Va.		
	James A. Meanley	12	M			Va.		
	Otway P. Marshall	29	M	Carpenter		Va.		
131	Henry D. Hankins	25	M	Farming		Va.		
	Lucy M. Hankins	26	F			Va.		
	Rebecca Hix	12	F			Va.		
	Cleopatra L. Hapkins	2	F			Va.		
132	Jno. M. Timberlake	27	M	Farming	1,500	Va.		
	Eliza Timberlake	29	F			Va.		
	Edgar Timberlake	4	M			Va.		
	Josephine Timberlake	2	F			Va.		
133	Philip(Philn) C. Jones	45	M	Farming	2,500	Va.		
	Martha A. Jones	37	F			Va.		
	Albina R. Jones	17	F			Va.		
	Wm. N. Jones	14	M			Va.		
	Ellen T. Jones	13	F			Va.		
	Martha V. R. Jones	6	F			Va.		
	Lucy Turner	61	F			Va.		
	Nath'l. I. Turner	35	M	none		Va.		
	Thos. I. Turner	33	M	none		Va.		
134	Chesley M. Jones	24	M	Farming		Va.	1	
	Martha L. Jones	22	F			Va.	1	
	Wm. T. Jones	22	M	none		Va.		
135	Daniel M. Jones	33	M	Farming	1,875	Va.		
	Benj. Chapman	55	M	none		N. J.		
136	Reuben Burnett	56	M	Farming	100	Va.		
	Peyton Burnett	23	M	Farming		Va.		
	James Burnett	19	M	Farming		Va.		
	Sarah Burnett	40	F			Va.		1
	Kitty Burnett	30	F			Va.		1
137	Chesley R. Jones	48	M	Farming	600	Va.		
	Delia Jones	40	F			Va.		
	William Jones	21	M	Carpenter		Va.		
	Ann Jones	18	F			Va.		
	Lewis Jones	16	M			Va.		
	Octavia Jones	14	F			Va.		
	Pamelia Jones	12	F			Va.		
138	War. M. Woodward	32	M	Farming	800	Va.		
	Mary A. Woodward	35	F			Va.		
	Mary A. B. Woodward	38	F			Va.		
	Geo. P. Ball	15	M	none		Va.		
	Ellen Woodward	8	F			Va.		
139	Wyatt S. Woodward	35	M	Farming	1,500	Va.		
	Frances Barham	58	F		350	Va.		
	Martha Woodward	24	F			Va.		

No of Family	Name	Age	Sex	Occupation	Value of Real Estate	Birth Place	Married within the Yr.	Over 20 & illiterate
128	Frances Woodward	6	F			Va.		
	Wyatt, F. Woodward	4	M			Va.		
	Martha Woodward	2	F			Va.		
140	Wm. A. Blayton	27	M	Woodcutter	$75	Va.		
141	James W. Timberlake	24	M	Farming	2,000	Va.		
	Sally Timberlake	56	F			Va.		
	Eliz. P. Timberlake	23	F			Va.		
	Sarah F. Timberlake	18	F			Va.		
	Melville, F. Timberlake	8/12	M			Va.		
142	Ro. S. Jennings	27	M	Farming	300	Va.		
	Susan Jennings	24	F			Va.		
	Mary B. Jennings	5	F			Va.		
	Sarah I. Jennings	3	F			Va.		
	Sarah Evans	25	F			Va.		
143	Wm. J. Bingley	37	M	Farming	300	Va.		
	Eliza. Bingley	27	F			Va.		
	James Bingley	11	M			Va.		
	Eliz. Bingley	6	F			Va.		
	Virginia Bingley	3	F			Va.		
	John Bingley	1	M			Va.		
144	Dudley Williams	64	M	Farming	400	Va.		
	Nancy Williams	50	F			Va.		
	Mary A. Williams	30	F			Va.		
	Delila Williams	19	F			Va.		
	Susan A. Williams	17	F			Va.		
	Isham Williams	16	M	none		Va.		
	Ben W. Williams	14	M			Va.		
	Harriet Williams	10	M			Va.		
145	Jno. P. Harman	49	M	Farming	100	Va.		
	Mary Harman	42	F			Va.		
	James Harman	16	M	none		Va.		
	Josiah Harman	10	M			Va.		
146	Wilson J. Tyree	55	M	Farming		Va.		1
	Christianna Tyree	37	F			Va.		1
	Harriet Tyree	11	F			Va.		
	Sheppard Tyree	10	M			Va.		
	Augusta Tyree	9	F			Va.		
	William Tyree	5	M			Va.		
	Betsey Tyree	3	F			Va.		
	Maria Tyree	1	F			Va.		
	Wm Finley	37	M	Collier		N. J.		
147	Archer Knewstep	72	M	Farming	300	Va.		
	Ann Knewstep	40	F			Va.		
	John W. Diggs	35	M.	Carpenter		Va.		
	Thos. A. Diggs	43	M	none		Va.		
148	Avery G. Farinholt	32	M	Farming	1,000	Va.		
	Eliz. Farinholt	35	F.			Va.		
	Alonzo Tyree	13	M			Va.		
	Mary E. Farinholt	8	F			Va.		
149	Jno. T. Merriman	23	M	Carpenter		Va	1	
	Martha I. Merriman	16	F			Va.	1	

No. of Family	Name	Age	Sex	Occupation	Value of Real Estate	Birth Place	Married within the Yr.	Over 20 & illiterate
138	Nancy Merriman	52	F		$100	Va.		
150	Jos. C. Hubbard	24	M	none		Va.		
151	Frances Bailey	43	F			Va.		
	Turner Atkinson	39	M	Farming		Va.		
	Eliz. R. Bailey	14	F			Va.		
	John Wood	70	M	Painting		Va.		
156	Pamelia L. Dungee	38	F			Va.		
	Lucy A. Hubbard	19	F.			Va.		
	Pamelia F. Hubbard	12	F			Va.		
	Bowler Hubbard	11	M			Va.		
	Wm. N. Hubbard	9	M			Va.		
	Benj. C. Hubbard	7	M			Va.		
	Jno. S. Hubbard	4	M			Va.		
157	Sheppard Hix	41	M	Merchant		Va.		1
	Eliz. Hix	41	F			Va.		
	Mary Hix	12	F			Va.		
	Sheppard Hix	6	M			Va.		
158	Garland A. Burnett	50	M	Farming	30	Va.	1	
	Levinia Burnett	30	F			Va.	1	
	James Burnett	22	M	none		Va.		
	John Burnett	19	M	none		Va.		
	Jenetta Howle	17	F			Va.		
	Julia A. Burnett	2/12	F			Va.		
159	Joseph Batkins	19	M	none		Va.		
	Betsey Batkins	50	F.			Va.		1
	Betsey Wade	30	F			Va.		1
161	Wm P. Pomfrey	34	M	Merchant		Va.		
	Elvira Pomfrey	75	F			Va.		
	Eliz. S. Pomfrey	24	F			Va.		
	Susan Howle	22	F			Va.		1
	Wm. P. Pomfrey	7	M			Va.		
	Betty Pomfrey	1	F			Va.		
	Mary S. Pomfrey	2/12	F			Va.		
162	John W. Howle	23	M	none		Va.	1	
	Delia A. Howle	21	F			Va.	1	
163	Frances B. Crump	51	F		2,000	Va.		
	Margaret B. Crump	26	F			Va.		
	William Crump	21	M	none		Va.		
	Bartler Crump	17	M	none		Va.		
	Burton Crump	16	M	none		Va.		
	Martha Crump	14	F			Va.		
	George Crump	10	M			Va.		
164	Mary Davis	45	F		1,500	Va.		
	Sarah Wade	35	F			Va.		
	Hugh L. Davis	20	M	Farming		Va.		
	Thos W. Davis	14	M			Va.		
	Frances E. Davis	12	F			Va.		

Page 28

No. of Family.	Name	Age	Sex.	Occu-pation.	Value of Real Estate	Birth-Place	Married within the Yr.	Over 20 & illit-erate.
165	Wm. W. Burnett	23	M	Farming		Va.		
	John Wright	59	M	None		Va.		
166	Wm. M. Garnett	45	M	Farming		Va.		
	Ro. A. Garnett	12	M			Va.		
	Cath. B. Garnett	7	F	7		Va.		
	Cath. C. Garnett	46	F			Va.		
167	Mary Crump	58	F		$1,000	Va.		
168	David. S. M. Crump	50	M	Farming	3,500	Va.		
	Mary A. Crump	34	F			Va.		
	Edgar M. Crump	16	M	none		Va.		
	Lawrence S. Crump	14	M			Va.		
	Annette Crump	10	F			Va.		
	Alice A. Crump	8	F			Va.		
	David W. Crump	6	M			Va.		
	Jno. S. Crump	3	M			Va.		
	Eliz. E. Crump	7/12	F			Va.		
169	Dand: W. Clarke	43	M	Farming	450	Va.		1
	Martha R. Clarke	47	F			Va.		
	Susan E. Clarke	20	F			Va.		
	Wm. A. Clarke	18	M	none		Va.		
	Major And. Clarke	16	M	none		Va.		
	Ro. Dand: Clarke	14	M	none		Va.		
	Martha R. Clarke	13	F			Va.		
	Lotsey F. Clarke	11	F			Va.		
	Harriet S. Clarke	10	F			Va.		
	George W. Clarke	9	M			Va.		
	Mary W. Clarke	5	F			Va.		
	Fred W. Clarke	3	M			Va.		
	Alice J. Clarke	1	F			Va.		
	John Clarke	30	M	Carpenter		Va.		
170	John Williams	65	M	Farming	1,600	Va.		
	Cynthia Williams	60	F			Va.		
	John Williams	24	M	Farming		Va.		
	Minerva Williams	25	F			Va.		
	Sarah A. Williams	8/12	F			Va.		
	Patsey Williams	87	F			Va.		
171	Raleigh P. Moore	31	M	Farming	500	Va.		
	Elizabeth Moore	28	F			Va.		
	John Moore	5	M			Va.		
	Walter Moore	1	M			Va.		
172	Ro. A. Farinholt	33	M	Farming	3,000	Va.		
	Harriet Farinholt	29	F			Va.		
	John Farinholt	8	M			Va.		
	Luther Farinholt	7	M			Va.		
	Louisa Farinholt	5	F			Va.		
	Ro. A. Farinholt	2	M			Va.		
	Geo. L. Farinholt	29	M	none		Va.		
173	Ed. B. Lacy	38	M	Farming	1,800	Va.		
	Harriet Lacy	37	F			Va.		

No. of Family	Name	Age	Sex	Occupation	Value of Real Estate	Birth-Place	Married within the Yr.	Over 20 & illiterate
174	Turner Richardson	49	M	Farming	$1,500	Va.		
	Margaret A. Richardson	29	F			Va.		
	Wm. A. Richardson	24	M	none		Va.		
	Harriet Richardson	25	F			Va.		
	Margaret Moore	19	F			Va.		
	David Richardson	5	M			Va.		
	Jos. M. Richardson	3	M			Va.		
	Senora Richardson	2	F			Va.		
	Ann E. Richardson	8/12	F			Va.		
175	John Hix	43	M	Farming		Va.		1
	Susan Hix	35	F			Va.		1
	Andrew Hix	11	M			Va.		
	Wm. M. Hix	10	M			Va.		
	Susan Hix	6	F			Va.		
	Mary F. Hix	3	F			Va.		
	Jno. R. Hix	1	M			Va.		
176	James Richardson	59	M	Farming	600	Va.		
	Jno. M. Richardson	22	M	Farming		Va.		
	Harriet B. Richardson	14	F			Va.		
	Ann E. Richardson	8	F			Va.		
	Addison F. Richardson	6	M			Va.		
	Joseph O. Richardson	1	M			Va.		
177	James M. Howard	33	M	Farming	200	Va.		
	Eliz. I. Howard	23	F			Va.		
	Wm. H. Howard	2	M			Va.		
178	Wm. H. Farthing	44	M	Farming		Va.		
	Susan W. Farthing	27	F			Va.		
	Maria L. Farthing	20	F			Va.		
	Mahala F. Farthing	17	F			Va.		
	Garico. H. Farthing	10	F			Va.		
	Presiosa E. Farthing	6	F			Va.		
	Inez R. Farthing	2	F			Va.		
	James S. Tyree	20	M	none		Va.		1
	Wm. Breeding	16	M	none		Va.		
179	Wm. Hill	34	M	Farming	4,000	Va.		
	Elizabeth Hill	25	F			Va.		
	John G. Hill	10	M			Va.		
	Julia A. Hill	5	F			Va.		
	Jas. M. Hill	3	M			Va.		
	Julian A. Hill	1	M			Va.		
180	H. D. Vaiden	33	M	Farming	1,500	Va.		
	Sarah M. Vaiden	24	F			Va.		
	Algernon Vaiden	3	M			Va.		
	Lucy O. Vaiden	2/12	F			Va.		
182	Joseph Glazebrook	24	M	Farming		Va.		1
	Maria Ison	45	F			Va.		1
	Wm. Ison	20	M	none		Va.		
	Ro. Ison	16	M	none		Va.		

Page 30

No. of Family	Name	Age	Sex	Occu-pation	Value of Real Estate	Birth-Place	Married within the Yr.	Over 20 & illit-erate
184	Daniel Robbins	54	M	Farming	$800	Va.		1
	Harriet Robbins	30	F			Va.		
	Daniel Robbins	13	M			Va.		
	Wm. Robbins	11	M			Va.		
	Eliza Robbins	9	F			Va.		
	Benj. Robbins	8	M			Va.		
	Sarah Robbins	5	F			Va.		
	Thomas Robbins	2	M			Va.		
	Joseph Robbins	6	M			Va.		
185	James Richardson	31	M	Physician	800	Va.		
	Mary G. Richardson	31	F			Va.		
	Alva S. Richardson	5	M			Va.		
	James L. Richardson	3	M			Va.		
	Mary A. Richardson	1	F			Va.		
186	Josiah Foster	31	M	Tailor	50	Va.		
	Rachael G. Foster	33	F			Va.		
	James Enos	19	M	none		Va.		
	Sarah E. Foster	4	F			Va.		
	W. M. L. Foster	3	M			Va.		
187	James Parrish	52	M	Farming	1,600	Va.		
	Mary R. Parrish	60	F			Va.		
188	John H. Mullen	30	M	Shoemaker		Va.	1	
	Celia Mullen	19	F			Va.	1	
189	Ro. S. Apperson	43	M	Physician	1,000	Va.		
	Martha A. M. Apperson	30	F			Va.		
	Eliz. W. Hockaday	44	F			Va.		
	William Hix	15	M	none		Va.		
	Richard C. Apperson	11	M	none		Va.		
	Ann R. Apperson	9	F			Va.		
	Maria B. Apperson	8	F			Va.		
	Martha L. Apperson	6	F			Va.		
	Mary L. Apperson	4	F			Va.		
	Eliz. M. Apperson	2/12	F			Va.		
190	Eliz. A. Bradenham	40	F		1,500	Va.		
	Mary Sherman	60	F			Va.		
*	Eliza Bradenham	50	F			Va.		
	Jno. R. Bradenham	10	M			Va.		
	Eliza A. Bradenham	6	F			Va.		
	James E. Bradenham	4	M			Va.		
	Mary R. Bradenham	11/12	F			Va.		
	James R. Taylor	36	M	Carpenter	400	Va.		
191	David Williams	68	M	Farming	2,000	Va.		
195	Jno. W. Richardson	37	M	Farming		Va.		
	Adeline Richardson	27	F			Va.		
	William Richardson	13	M			Va.		
	Louisa Richardson	9	F			Va.		
	Eliz. Richardson	6	F			Va.		
	Jno. W. Richardson	2	M			Va.		
197	Sam'l C. Wright	39	M	Farming		Va.		1

Page 31

No. of Family	Name	Age	Sex.	Occupation	Value of Real Estate	Birth-place.	Married within the Yr.	Over 20 && illiterate
	Sarah Wright	45	F			Va.		
	Harriet Breeding	17	F			Va.		
	Mary A. Richardson	17	F			Va.		
198	Amanda B. Knewstep	39	F		$2,000	Va.		
	Lucy M. Knewstep	17	F.			Va.		
	William S. Knewstep	12	M			Va.		
	Miles Knewstep	7	M			Va.		
	Leonida Knewstep	3	M			Va.		
	Harriet Knewstep	1	F			Va.		
	Alice Hix	22	F			Va.		1
199	Jno. Dunsford	58	M	Farming	800	Va.		
	Rebecca Dunsford	52	F			Va.		
	Mary Dunsford	18	F			Va.		
	Emily Dunsford	13	F			Va.		
	Mary Robbins	4	F			Va.		
	Jno. E. Dunsford	30	M	none		Va.		
	Matilda Dunsford	30	F			Va.		
	Wm. Richardson	19	M	none		Va.		
	Mary C. Dunsford	1	F			Va.		
200	Archer R. Mitchell	56	M	Farming	500	Va.		
	Mary Mitchell	52	F			Va.		
	Martha Mitchell	22	F			Va.		
	Geo. W. Mitchell	24	M	none		Va.		
	James M. Mitchell	18	M	none		Va.		
	John E. Mitchell	15	M	none		Va.		
	Sarah S. Mitchell	14	F			Va.		
201	Eliza Hockaday	33	F		500	Va.		
	Judith W. Hockaday	13	F			Va.		
	Jno.R. Hockaday	10	M			Va.		
	Sarah C. Hockaday	9	F			Va.		
	Eliza A. Hockaday	2	F			Va.		
202	Jno. G. Mitchell	53	M	Farming	400	Va.		
	Eliza W. Mitchell	26	F			Va.		
	Martha Casey	30	F			Va.		1
	Peter G. Mitchell	4	M			Va.		
203	Wm. A. Mitchell	27	M	Farming	30	Va.		
	Sarah C. Mitchell	26	F			Va.		1
	Mary Hockaday	21	F			Va		
	Richard W. Hockaday	1	M			Va.		
204	Geo. W. Morriss	33	M	Doctor		Va.		
	Anna F. Morriss	25	F			Va.		
	Rebecca Morriss	64	F			Va.		
	Mary F. Marston	16	F			Va.		
	Wm. W. Marston	13	M			Va.		
	Wm. N. Morriss	3	M			Va.		
	Geo. W. Morriss	2	M			Va.		
	David S. M. Morriss	1	M			Va.		

Page 32-

No. of Family	Name	Age	Sex.	Occupation	Value of Real Estate	Birth-Place	Married within the Yr.	Over 20 & illiterate
205	Geo. W. Richardson	46	M	Farming	$3,500	Va.		
	Martha Richardson	23	F			Va.		
	William Richardson	20	M	none		Va.		
	Octavia Richardson	14	F			Va.		
	Geo. W. Richardson	10	M			Va.		
	Aug. Richardson	8	M			Va.		
	Colus Richardson	5	M			Va.		
	Susan Richardson	4	F			Va.		
	Virginia Richardson	2	F			Va.		
206	Cornelius Filbates	23	M	Farming	8,000	Va.		
	Walker Lightfoot	24	M	none		Va.		
	Harriet L. Filbates	17	F			Va.		
	Elenora Filbates	7/12	F			Va.		
	Wm. Lightfoot	24	M	none		Va.		
207	Leroy Williams	52	M	Farming	800	Va.		
	Susan Williams	37	F			Va.		
	Lucy Filbates	14	F			Va.		
	Ellen H. Williams	7	F			Va.		
209	Wm. O. Hockaday	25	M	Farming		Va.		
	Mary B. Hockaday	24	F			Va.		
	Eliz. R. Hockaday	7/12	F			Va.		
210	Sarah Hockaday	48	F			Va.		
	Jno. A. Hockaday	13	M			Va.		
	James Robbins	9	M			Va.		
211	James N. Goddin	32	M	Farming	1,800	Va.		
	Mary A. Goddin	29	F			Va.		
	Sylvanus Goddin	5	M			Va.		
	James H. Goddin	4	M			Va.		
	Geo. P. Goddin	1	M			Va.		
213	Benj. Vaiden	18	M	Merchant		Va.		
219	Mary H. Richardson	57	F		4,000	Va.		
	Delia Jones	24	F			Va.		
	Cath. E. Ratcliffe	21	F			Va.		
	Ange. T. Richardson	18	F			Va.		
	Theo. Richardson	14	M			Va.		
	Sylvester H. Richardson	10	M			Va.		
	Cornelia Jones	3	F			Va.		
220	Selden C. Slater	21	M	Merchant	50	Va.		
	And. P. Richardson	21	M	Merchant		Va.		
221	Spencer Jennings	50	M	Farming	800	Va.		1
	Martha A. Jennings	46	F			Va.		
	Major R. Jennings	17	M	none		Va.		
	Emiley S. Jennings	15	F			Va.		
	John W. Jennings	12	M			Va.		
	Martha A. Jennings	11	F			Va.		
	Laura F. Jennings	8	F			Va.		
	Geo. W. Jennings	7	M			Va		
	James K. P. Jennings	5	M			Va.		

No. of Family	Name	Age	Sex	Occu-pation	Value of Real Estate	Birth-Place	Married within the Yr.	Over 20 & illit-erate
222	Ro. S. Jennings-	30	M	Farming		Va.		
	Mary T. Jennings	44	F			Va.		1
	William Hix	19	M			Va.		
	Ahaz Hix	11	M			Va.		
223	Wm. A. Fiddler	33	M	none		Va.	1	
	Mary A. E. Fiddler	23	F			Va.	1	
	Matilda Bernard	33	F			Va.		
224	Wm. M. Goodman	29	M	none		Va.		
	Virginia A. Goodman	27	F			Va.		
	Angelica Goodman	7	F			Va.		
	Sarah E. Goodman	5	F			Va.		
	Wm. H. Goodman	3	M			Va.		
	Jno. H. Goodman	1	M			Va.		
225	Ro. W. H. Atkinson	36	M	Farming	$500	Va.		
	Eliza R. Atkinson	26	F			Va.		
	Jno J. Atkinson	5	M			Va.		
	Henry W. Atkinson	3	M			Va.		
	Frances A. Atkinson	1	F			Va.		
226	Sarah Crump	45	F		700	Va.		
	Lemuel Crump	13	M			Va.		
	Hammond F. Crump	9	M			Va.		
227	Eliz. Hilliard	49	F		250	Va.		
	Isaac M. Hilliard	23	M	Farming		Va.		
228	Mary A. Clarke	37	F			Va.		
	Jno. O. Clarke	15	M	none		Va.		
	Rebecca Clarke	12	F			Va.		
	Eliz. C. Clarke	10	F			Va.		
	Jas. W. Clarke	8	M			Va.		
	And. W. Clarke	6	M			Va.		
	Mary E. Clarke	4	F			Va.		
	Ro. S. Clarke	2	M			Va.		
229	Mary A.E. Chandler	44	F			Va.		
	Mary A.W. Chandler	14	F			Va.		
	Georgianna W. Chandler	11	F			Va.		
	Miles M. Chandler	7	M			Va.		
230	Eliza Meredith	53	F		800	Va.		
	Susan B. Meredith	53	F		150	Va.		
	Susan Austin	40	F			Va.		1
	Eliza Dudley	34	F			Va.		
	Hannah Meredith	12	F			Va.		
231	Ro. F. Meredith	25	M	Merchant		Va.		
	Sam'l. A. Meredith	22	M	Merchant		Va.		
	Eugene Sullivan	17	M	none		Va.		
	Allen W. Borvis?	40	M	Carpenter		Va.		
232	James S. Atkinson	43	M	Carpenter		Va.		
	Mary W. Atkinson	44	F			Va.		
	Georgianna Atkinson	9	F			Va.		
	Mary E. Atkinson	6	F			Va.		
	Rebecca Atkinson	5	F			Va.		
	Jno. S. Curle	4	M			Va.		

Page 34

No. of Family	Name	Age	Sex	Occupation	Value of Real Estate	Birth Place	Married within the Yr.	Over 20 & illiterate
234	Richard S. Wilkes	37	M	Wheelright	$300	Va.		
	Sarah A. Wilkes	36	F			Va.		
	William Wilkes	8	M			Va.		
	George Wilkes	3	M			Va.		
235	Mary E. Stewart	40	F			Va.		
	Ann. E. Stewart	21	F			Va.		
	Ro. F. Stewart	15	M	none		Va.		
	Mary V. Stewart	7	F			Va.		
	Josephine Stewart	4	F			Va.		
	Maria L. Stewart	4	F			Va.		
236	Pat. H. Crump	43	M	none	100	Va.		
	Eliz. S. Crump	43	F			Va.		
	Jno. W. Crump	16	M	none		Va.		
237	Jno. Ball	60	M	Farming	1,500	Va.		
	Eliza. Ball	55	F			Va.		
	Elizabeth Vaughan	16	F			Va.		
	Indianna Ball	14	F			Va.		
	Walter Ball	6	M			Va.		
	Perrien Ball	4	F			Va.		
238	Jno. F. Woodward	32	M	Farming	1,500	Va.		
	Nancy Woodward	29	F			Va.		
	Wm. Woodward	8	M			Va.		
	Virginia Woodward	5	F			Va.		
239	Thos. S. Martin	37	M	Farming	1,500	Va.		
	Harriet Martin	28	F			Va.		
	Betsy Lester	60	F			Va.		
	Jos. H. Woodward	23	M			Va.		
	Richard G. Woodward	20	M	none		Va.		
	Alcesta Martin	8	F			Va.		
	Virginia Martin	6	F			Va.		
	William Martin	2	M			Va.		
240	Wm D. C. Wade	35	M	Farming		Va.		
	Cath. M. Wade	33	F			Va.		
	Ann E. Wade	13	F			Va.		
	Wm. T. Wade	11	M			Va.		
	Jas. H. Wade	9	M			Va.		
	Maria D. Wade	6	F			Va.		
	Ro. W. Wade	4	M			Va.		
	Mary S. W. Wade	1	F			Va.		
241	Jno. M. Sweeney	41	M	Farming	600	Va.		
	Eliz. U. Sweeney	38	F			Va.		
	Frances R. Woodward	65	F			Va.		
	Frances Woodward	34	F			Va.		
	Martha Woodward	31	F			Va.		
	Minerva Woodward	27	F			Va.		
	Martha Sweeney	17	F			Va.		
	Sarah Sweeney	15	F			Va.		
	Martha Hughes	15	F			Va.		
	Richardson F. Sweeney	14	M			Va.		

No. of Family	Name	Age	Sex	Occupation	Value of Real Estate	Birth Place	Married within the Yr.	Over 20 & illiterate
?	Stephen B. Sweeney	13	M			Va.		
	Nancy Hughes	13	F			Va.		
	Stephen B. Sweeney	13	M			Va.		
	Mary F. Sweeney	10	F			Va.		
	Chas. H. Sweeney	9	M			Va.		
	Jos. W. Sweeney	3	M			Va.		
	Maria L. Sweeney	1	F			Va.		
242	Wm. Ratcliffe	62	M	Farming	$900	Va.		
	Mary A. Ratcliffe	52	F			Va.		
	Lucy A. Ratcliffe	20	F			Va.		
	Martha A. Ratcliffe	18	F			Va.		
	Judith W. Ratcliffe	16	F			Va.		
	Wm. T. Ratcliffe	13	M			Va.		
243	Joel W. Eames	48	M	Farming	800	Va.		
	Frances Eames	52	F			Va.		
	James L. Eames	13	M			Va.		
244	Benskin M. Hilliard	45	M	Farming		Va.		
	Cynthia Hilliard	40	F		800	Va.		
	Julia Roper	10	F			Va.		
	Wm. E. Hilliard	5	M			Va.		
	Jno. H. Timberlake	26	M	none		Va.		1
245	Judith Eames	47	F			Va.		
	Pleasant W. Eames	16	M	none		Va.		
	Letter Eames	20	F			Va.		
246	D.N. Jones	30	M	Farming	600	Va.		
	Leuversa Jones	34	F			Va.		
	Martha A. Jones	26	F			Va.		
	James Jones	24	M	none		Va.		
	William Jones	22	M	none		Va.		
	Nancy Jones	18	F			Va.		
	Eliza Jones	15	F			Va.		
247	Randolph Jones	60	M	Farming		Va.		1d
	Rebecca Jones	3	F			Va.		
	Micajah Harman	16	M	none		Va.		
248	Jane Mills	27	F			Va.		
	Mary E. Mills	7	F			Va.		
	Jno. A. Mills	5	M			Va.		
	Cynthia E. Mills	4	F			Va.		
	Emiley A. Mills	1	F			Va.		
249	Fred. Kirkmyer	35	M	Sailor	300	Va.		
	Eliz. Kirkmyer	15	F			Va.		
	George Kirkmyer	10	M			Va.		
	Wm. Kirkmyer	8	M			Va.		
	Fred. C. Kirkmyer	4	M			Va.		
250	James A. Williams	36	M	Farming	1,000	Va.		
	Octavia S. Williams	22	F			Va.		
	Mortimer Williams	11	M			Va.		
	Virginia Williams	7	F			Va.		
	Augustus Williams	2	M			Va.		
251	Chesley Jones	70	M	Farming	3,000	Va.		

No. of Family	Name	Age	Sex	Occupation	Value of Real Estate	Birthplace	Married within the Yr.	Over 20 & illiterate
	Eliza Jones	50	F			Va.		
	Vernon Jones	21	M	none		Va.		
	Burwell B. Jones	17	M	none		Va.		
	Maria Jones	12	F			Va.		
	Willentina Jones	8	F			Va.		
252	Jno. S. Lacy	40	M	Farming	$3,000	Va.		
	Jno. B. Lacy	14	M			Va.		
	Sally H. Lacy	9	F			Va.		
253	James Evans	28	M	Farming		Va.	1	
	Nancy Evans	26	F			Va.	1	
	Mary A. W. Evans	2	F			Va.		
254	Wm. Filbates	55	M	Farming	300	Va.		1
	Mary Filbates	45	F			Va.		1
	Wm. Filbates Jr.	22	M	none		Va.		1
	Mary Filbates	18	F			Va.		
	Tho. Filbates	15	M	none		Va.		
	Benj. Filbates	12	M			Va.		
255	Henry L. Pond	49	M	Farming	125	Va.		
	Frances Pond	47	F			Va.		1
	Emeline W. Pond	14	F			Va.		
256	Jno. A. Richardson	24	M	Merchant		Va.		
	Ann E. Richardson	23	F			Va.		
	Geo. N. Richardson 9/	12	M			Va.		
257	Frances H. Timberlake	56	F			Va.		
	Wm. I Timberlake	32	M	Farming		Va.		
	James A. Timberlake	29	M	none		Va.		
	Jno. C. Timberlake	22	M	none		Va.		
	Benj. N. Timberlake	15	M	none		Va.		
	Geo. A. Timberlake	13	M			Va.		
	Eliz. Hix	15	F			Va.		
	Jno. I. Garrett	11	M			Va.		
258	Benj. Timberlake	47	M	Farming	2,000	Va.		
	Eliza S. Timberlake	43	F			Va.		
	Mary E. Timberlake	19	F			Va.		
	Eliza T Timberlake	17	F			Va.		
	Courtney T. Timberlake	15	F			Va.		
	Jas B. Timberlake	11	M			Va.		
	Virga. C. Timberlake	5	F			Va.		
	Margt. W. Timberlake	1	F			Va.		
259	Susan B. Taylor	42	F		300	Va.		
	Elizabeth Taylor	18	F			Va.		
	James Taylor	16	M	none		Va.		
	Abner Taylor	4	M			Va.		
260	Eliza A. Tyree	36	F			Va.		
	Jno. C. Tyree	5	M			Va.		
	Leonidas R. Tyree	3	M			Va.		
	Wm. C. Tyree	1	M			Va.		
	Nancy Hix	64	F			Va.		
261	Wm. N. Cumber	28	M	none		Va.		1
	Cynthia Hix	50	F			Va		1
	Rebecca Hix	48	F			Va.		1
	A. Taylor	23	F			Va.		1
	Sophia T. Cumber	22	F			Va.		

No. of Family	Name	Age	Sex	Occupation	Value of Real Estate	Birth-Place	Married within The Yr.	Over 20 & illiterate
261	Savannah W. Cumber	4	F			Va.		
	Thos. E. Cumber	2	M			Va.		
262	Jno. H. Walker	56	M	Farming	$600	Va.		
	Lucy R. Walker	58	F			Va.		
263	Chs. R. Jones	34	M	Farming	400	Va.		
	Druscilla B. Jones	29	F			Va.		
	Wm A. Jones	5	M			Va.		
	Amanda B. Jones	3	F			Va.		
	Frances R. Jones	2	F			Va.		
	Lucy A. Jones	4/12	F			Va.		
264	Benj. F. Lester	50	M	Farming	900	Va.		
	Lucy R. Lester	29	F			Va.		
	John B. Lester	3	M			Va.		
265	Lydia Ratcliff	52	F			Va.		
	Adeline Ratcliff	32	F			Va.		
	Nancy Ratcliff	21	F			Va.		
266	James A. Stewart	27	M	Farming	100	Va.		1
	Rebecca Stewart	30	F			Va.		1
	Sarah Stewart	30	F			Va.		
	Christianna Stewart	11	F			Va.		
	Sarah A. Curle	5	F			Va.		
	Hester A. Boswell	4	F			Va.		
	Wm. T. Curle	2	M			Va.		
267	Rowland Jones	53	M	Farming	1500	Va.		
	Lucy B. Jones	49	F			Va.		
	H. B. Jones	28	M	Merchant		Va.		
	Martha W. Jones	26	F			Va.		
	Rowland A. Jones	4	M			Va.		
	Lucy C. Jones	2	F			Va.		
268	Wm. H. Woodward	42	M	Wheelright	400	Va.		
	Mary Woodward	38	F			Va.		
	Robert Woodward	12	M			Va.		
	Wm. H. Woodward	11	M			Va.		
	Harrison Woodward	9	M			Va.		
	Lemuel Woodward	7	M			Va.		
	Ann E. Woodward	5	F			Va.		
	Harman Woodward	2	M			Va.		
	Eliz. Woodward	11	F			Va.		
269	David Timberlake	58	M	Farming	150	Va.		
	Eliz. Timberlake	51	F			Va.		1
	David Timberlake	17	M			Va.		
	Wm. H. Timberlake	13	M			Va.		
270	Mary Timberlake	61	F		150	Va.	1	
	David Timberlake	39	M	Farming		Va.	1	
	Julia A. Stewart	25	F			Va.	1	
	Richard Stewart	25	M	none		Va.	1	
	Haman Timberlake	20	M	none		Va.	1	
	Maria L. Timberlake	18	F			Va.		
	Elija F. Timberlake	12	M			Va.		
	Wyatt Stewart	3/12	M			Va.		
271	Abner Wilkes	40	M	Farming	500	Va.		
	Mary R. Wilkes	30	F			Va.		
	Martha E. Wilkes	12	F			Va.		
	Chs. T. Wilkes	10	M			Va.		

No. of Family	Name	Age	Sex	Occupation	Value of Real Estate	Birthplace	Married within the Yr.	Over 20 & illiterate
	Louisianna Wilkes	8	F			Va.		
	Selden Wilkes	6	M			Va.		
	Rebecca Wilkes	4	F			Va.		
	Wilkes	3/12	F			Va.		
272	James G. Otey	54	M	Farming	200	Va.		
	Sarah W. Otey	47	F			Va.		
	Mary Otey	21	F			Va.		
	Lucy A. Otey	13	F			Va.		
	Wm. R. Otey	10	M			Va.		
	Martha R. Otey	8	F			Va.		
	Sarah Otey	6	F			Va.		
	James A. Otey	3	M			Va.		
273	George Crump	50	M	Farming	150	Va		1
	Martha Crump	30	F			Va		
	Jo I. Crump	40	M	Schoolmaster		Va.		
	George Crump	10	M			Va.		
	Elizabeth Crump	20	F			Va.		
	Jos. T. P. Crump	16	M			Va.		
	William Crump	8	M			Va.		
	Sarah Crump	5	F			Va.		
	John Crump	2	M			Va.		
274	John Boswell	65	M	Farming	300	Va.		
	Lucy Boswell	58	F			Va.		
	Tabithy Boswell	23	F			Va.		
	Joseph Boswell	17	M			Va.		
	Edward Boswell	19	M			Va.		
	Mary F. Boswell	15	F			Va.		
275	Isaac Couch	33	M	Farming		New Jersey		
	Sarah A. Couch	29	F			New Jersey		
	Mary Couch	12	F			New Jersey		
	James W. Couch	10	M			New Jersey		
	John W. Couch	8	M			Va.		
	Ro. K. Couch	6	M			Va.		
	Emily Couch	2	F			Va.		
	Hester A. Couch	2	F			Va.		
276	Wm. B. Claiborne	54	M	none	100	Va.		
277	Sarah M. Vaughan	30	F			Va.		
	Jno. T. Vaughan	7	M			Va.		
	Susan E. Vaughan	3	F			Va.		
	Wm R. Vaughan	2	M			Va.		
278	Ann Browne	60	F			Va.		
	Susan Atkinson	30	F			Va.		
	Sally G. Atkinson	28	F			Va.		
279	Dianna Porter	44	F			Va.		
	Roscoe, T. Vaughan	27	M	none		Va.	1	
	James H. Porter	23	M	Carpenter	55	Va.		
	Eleanor Vaughan	21	F			Va.	1	
280	John Glenn	51	M	Farming		Va.		
	Eliz. Glenn	65	F			Va.		
	Mary Martin	30	F			Va.		
281	Richard Boswell	40	M	Farming	300	Va.		1
	Lucy J. Boswell	41	F			Va.		1
	Wm. J. Boswell	8	M			Va.		
	Martha. A. Boswell	6	F			Va.		

No. of Family	Name	Age	Sex	Occupation	Value of Real Estate	Birth place	Married within the Yr.	Over 20 & illiterate.
	John W. Boswell	4	M			Va.		
	Lucinda Boswell	2	F			Va.		
	_____ Boswell	2/12	F			Va.		
	Susan Taylor	23	F			Va.		1
282	Richard P. Cooke	37	M	Farming	3000	Va.		
	Sarah E. Cooke	30	F			Va.		
	Richard M. Timberlake	20	M	School Teacher		Va.		
	Jno. R. T. Porter	19	M	none		Va.		
	Margaret C. Cooke	13	F			Va.		
	Ann E. Cooke	12	F			Va.		
	Mary A. Cooke	10	F			Va.		
	Mary E. Cooke	9	F			Va.		
283	Robert B. Chandler	58	M	Farming	1500	Va.		
	James M. Appersen	26	M	Farming	415	Va.		
	Ann E. Apperson	24	F			Va.		
284	D. P. Chandler	27	M	Carpenter		Va.		
	Theo. L. Chandler	24	M	Farming	1000	Va.		
	Margaret Patterson	38	F			Va.		
	Margaret S. Patterson	4	F			Va.		
285	Elizabeth Odell	39	F			Va.		
	Sarah F. Odell	18	F			Va.		
	Thos M. Odell	14	M			Va.		
	Jno. D. Odell	10	M			Va.		
	Henry H. Odell	9	M			Va.		
	Margaret D. Odell	4	F			Va.		
286	Joseph Atkinson	57	M	Farming	150	Va.		
	Martha Atkinson	49	F			Va.		1
	John Atkinson	21	M			Va.		
	William Atkinson	12	M			Va.		
287	Martha M. Taylor	58	F			Va.		Pauper
	Eliz: Taylor	14	F			Va.		"
	Martha Taylor	11	F			Va.		"
	James Austin	30	M			Va.		
	Mary Austin	25	F			Va.		1
288	Wm. T. Sweeney	52	M	Farming	200	Va.		
290	Ira L. Bowles	42	M	Farming	4500	Va.		
292	James Austin	31	M	Farming		Va.		1
	Lucy Austin	31	F			Va.		1
	Henrietta Austin	3	F			Va.		
293	John Taylor	22	M	none		Va.	1	1
	Mary F. Austin	20	F			Va.	1	1
294	Sally Smith	45	F			Va.		1
	Ro. Smith	18	M	none		Va.		
	Ellen Smith	16	F			Va.		
	Charles Smith	12	M			Va.		
	James Smith	7	M			Va.		
295	Mary Call	44	F			Va.	Pauper	1
	Susan Call	23	F			Va.		1
	Eliz; Call	21	F			Va.		1
	Lewis Call	18	M	none		Va.		
	Mary Call	17	F			Va.		
	Wm. Call	14	M			Va.		
	Lucy A. Call	12	F			Va.		
	Sarah Boswell	33	F			Va.		1

Page 40

No. of Family	Name.	Age	Sex	Occupation	Value of Real Estate	Birth place	Married within the Yr.	Over 20 & illiterate
296	Wm. R. Eames	46	M	Farming		Va.		
	Emeline Eames	30	F			Va.		
	Jno. W. Eames	3	M			Va.		
	Octavia Eames	9/12	F			Va.		
297	Launcelot Austin	48	M	Carpenter		Va.		
	Rebecca Austin	40	F			Va.		1
	Christopher Austin	24	M			Va.		
	Thos. W. Austin	12	M			Va.		
	Geo. W. Austin	9	M			Va.		
	Wm. Austin	20	M	none		Va.		
	Delaware Austin	19	M	none		Va.		
298	Ro: T. Browne	32	M	Carpenter		Va.		1
	Jane Browne	28	F			Va.		
	Nancy Boswell	50	F			Va.		
	Mary E. Browne	6	F			Va.		
	Susan F. Browne	4	F			Va.		
	Octavia Browne	2	F			Va.		
299	Elizabeth Gilliam	40	F			Va.		1
	Elizabeth E. Gilliam	22	F			Va.		
	Ro: A. Gilliam	18	M	none		Va.		
	Rufus T. Gilliam	14	M			Va.		
	Martha I. W. Gilliam	12	F			Va.		
	Maria S. Gilliam	8	F			Va.		
	Eliz. F. Clarke	7	F			Va.		
300	Wm. A. Atkinson	55	M	Farming	200	Va.		
	Eliz: Atkinson	52	F			Va.		
	Ann M. Vaughan	40	F			Va.		
	Frances Atkinson	28	M	Cabinate maker		Va.		
	Lucy A. Atkinson	18	F			Va.		
	Richd. O. Atkinson	11	M			Va.		
	Susan A.E. Lacy	7	F			Va.		
301	Eliz: T. Mills	47	F			Va. pauper		1
	Emeline S. Southall	38	F			Va.		
	Mansfield Mills	15	M	none		Va.		
	Virginia Mills	20	F			Va. pauper		
	Martha J. Mills	9	F			Va. pauper		
302	George Stewart	21	M	none		Va.		
303	Eliza F. Sweeney	31	F			Va.		
	Mary Hughes	18	F			Va.		
	Jos. C. Sweeney	12	M			Va.		
	Minerva Sweeney	7	F			Va.		
305	Caroline Williams	32	F			Va.		
	Alexander Williams	3	M			Va.		
	Edward Williams	1	M			Va.		
	Wm. D. Williams	30	M	none		Va.		
306	Thos: Q. Gilliam	22	M	Merchant		Va.	1	1
	Frances A. Gilliam	24	F			Va.	1	
	Wm. O. Gilliam	14	M			Va.		
	Jos. C. Morriss	10	M			Va.		
307	Jno. S. Gilliam	57	M	none		Va.		
	Emeline C. Gilliam	19	F			Va.		
	James C. Gilliam	11	M			Va.		
	Patrickanna Morriss	3	F			Va.		

No. of Family	Name	Age	Sex	Occu- pation	Value of Real Estate	Birth- place	Mar- ried within the Yr.	Over 20 & illit- erate
308	Jno. O. Franks	35	M	Farming	$ 200	Va.	1	1
	Eliz; Franks	22	F			Va.	1	
	Martha Mills	58	F			Va.		1
309	Virginia Franks	22	F			Va.		1
	Amanda T. Franks	3	F			Va.		
	Jno. D. Franks	1	M			Va.		
310	Fanny Moore	38	F			Va.		
	Ann. E. Moore	8	F			Va.		
310	Ro: S. Taylor	27	M	Merchant	700	Va.		
312	Wm. A. Burnett	27	M	Farming		Va.		
	Lucy A. Burnett	25	F			Va.		
	Rebecca Franks	5	F			Va.		
	Sydney Burnett	4/12	M			Va.		
313	James Chandler	42	M	Farming		Va.		1
	Cath: Crump	60	F			Va.		1
	Mary A. Chandler	43	F			Va.		
	Wesley Gilliam	17	M	none		Va.		
	Jos. Chandler	12	M			Va.		
	Vandalia Chandler	8	F			Va.		
	Jno. F. Chandler	5	M			Va.		
314	Wm.H.Mills	55	M	Farming		Va.		1
	Frances T. Mills	44	F			Va.		
	Wm. P. Mills	20	M	none		Va.		
	Betty Mills	15	F			Va.		
	Archer W. Mills	10	M			Va.		
	Eugenia C.Mills	7	F			Va.		
315	Thos: Wright	38	M	Farming		Va.		1
	Ro: B. Wright	13	M			Va.		
	Mary A.E.T.Wright	12	F			Va.		
316	Richd. S. Gilliam	30	M	Farming		Va.		1
	Fanny Gilliam	28	F			Va.		1
	Eppa.D.Gilliam	4	M			Va.		
	Margaret J. Gilliam	2	F			Va.		
	Sarah F. Gilliam	1	F			Va.		
317	Richd. B.Taylor	37	M	Farming	600	Va.		
318	Thos: S. Morriss,Sr	60	M	Farming	1500	Va.		
	Mary A. Morriss	43	F			Va.		
319	Wm. C. Talley	37	M	Farming	1600	Va.		
	Lucy A. Talley	33	F			Va.		
	Richd. W. Talley	6	M			Va.		
	Nathl. C. Talley	1	M			Va.		
	Emeline E.Meanley	25	F			Va.		
322	Averilla Woodward	57	F			Va.	pauper	
	Susan Martin	20	F			Va.	pauper	
336	Richard Griggs	61	M	none	50	Va.	blind	1
	Mary Griggs	40	F			Va.		1
340	Betsy Martin	43	F			Va.		1
	Frances Martin	20	F			Va.		1
341	Lucy A. Wilkinson	60	F			Va.		
	Nancy Wilkinson	70	F			Va.		
	Frances E. Wilkinson	27	F			Va.		
342	Julius C. Dixon	33	M	Farming	300	Va.		1
	Elizabeth Porter	59	F			Va.		
	Mary C. Dixon	25	F			Va.		

Page 41

No. of Family	Name	Age	Sex	Occupation	Value of Real Estate	Birthplace	Married within the Yr.	Over 20 & illiterate
	William R. Dixon	6/12	M			Va.		
343	Zac: Shackelford	42	M	Farming	250	Va.		
	Richard Shackelford	40	M	Shoemaker		Va.		
	Mary Shackelford	23	F			Va.		
	John Shackelford	17	M	none		Va.		
	Lewellen Shackelford	14	M			Va.		
	Susan Shackelford	14	F			Va.		
	Ro: Leo Shackelford	3	M			Va.		
	Andrew Shackelford	5	M			Va.		
	Wm. H. Shackelford	4/12	M			Va.		
	Eneline Shackelford	16	F			Va.		
344	John G. Crump	46	M	Farming	3700	Va.		
	Mary Crump	35	F			Va.		
	Lucy P. Crump	18	F			Va.		
	Wm. B. Crump	16	M			Va.		
	Sylvanus G. Crump	14	M			Va.		
	George T. Crump	12	M			Va.		
	Mary F. Crump	10	F			Va.		
	Ann E. Crump	8	F			Va.		
	Maria S. Crump	3	F			Va.		
	Virginia B. Crump	1	F			Va.		
345	Orlanzo Lindsey	26	M	none		Va.		
346	O.P. Binns	38	M	Farming	1800	Va.		
	Amelia A.C. Binns	27	F			Va.		
	Ann K.C. Otey	42	F			Va.		
	Betty Lipscomb	14	F			Va.		
	Anna Otey	12	F			Va.		
	John Otey	11	M			Va.		
	Chs. D. Binns	7	M			Va.		
	Ambrose W. Binns	5	M			Va.		
	Frances C. Binns	3	F			Va.		
	O.P. Binns, Jr.	2/12	M			Va.		
347	William H. Vaiden	49	M	Farming	700	Va.		
	Eliza Vaiden	43	F			Va.		
	Isabella Vaiden	19	F			Va.		
	Virgillia Vaiden	18	F			Va.		
	Otelia Vaiden	15	F			Va.		
	Martha Vaiden	9	F			Va.		
	Eliza Vaiden	7	F			Va.		
	Margaret Vaiden	5	F			Va.		
348	Wm. S. Boswell	33	M	Farming	350	Va.		1
	Susanna Boswell	32	F			Va.		
	Nancy Goodman	56	F			Va.		
	John L. Boswell	6	M			Va.		
	Ann. E. Boswell	3	F			Va.		
	Mary E. Boswell	1	F			Va.		
349	Ballard Sherman	23	M	Farming	250	Va.		
	Eliza J. Sherman	24	F			Va.		
	Lucy H. Sherman	3	F			Va.		
	Richard A. Clarke	10	M			Va.		
	P. ..? W. Clarke	6	M			Va.		
350	Zac: Austin	44	M	Farming	150	Va.		
	Lucy Austin	38	F			Va		
	Jas. T. Austin	17	M			Va.		

No. of Family	Name	Age	Sex	Occupation	Value of Real Estate	Birth Place	Married within the Yr.	Over 20 & illiterate
	Mary A. E. Austin	14	F			Va.		
	Martha E. Austin	11	F			Va.		
	Leroy L. Austin	9	M			Va.		
351	Wm. M. Sherman	52	M	Farming	1500	Va.		
	Eliz: W. Sherman	51	F			Va.		
	Ro: M. Sherman	24	M	none		Va.		
	George W. Sherman	20	M	none		Va.		
352	Barnett Moore	78	M			Va. pauper		1
	Lucy Adams	20	F			Va		
	Judith Moore	23	F			Va.		1
353	Wm. G. Boswell	40	M	Farming	100	Va.		
	Jno. T. Boswell	10	M			Va.		
	Jas. W. Boswell	7	M			Va.		
	Eliz. Stroud	40	F			Va.		
354	Jas. C. Hazwell	40	M	Farming		Va.		1
	Mary F. Hazwell	30	F			Va.		1
	Washington Hazwell	12	M			Va.		
355	Wm. G. Harman? (Hannan?)	49	M	Farming	1500	Va.		
	Martha A. Harman	36	F			Va.		
	Richd. Crump	16	M			Va.		
	Ann W. Crump	14	F			Va.		
	Martha J. Harmon	13	F			Va.		
	Benj. Harmon	9	M			Va.		
	Sally H. Harman	6	F			Va.		
	Ann. E. Harman	4	F			Va.		
356	Mary E. Walker	43	F			Va.		
	Bens: H. Walker	24	M	Farming		Va.		
	Ro: H. Walker	21	M	none		Va.		
	Harman B. Walker	18	M	none		Va.		
	Jas. D. Walker	15	M	none		Va.		
	Mary A. Walker	10	F			Va.		
	Fanny B. Walker	6	F			Va.		
	Ro: C. Wilkins	35	M	Miller		Va.		
	Sarah Wilkins	27	F			Va.		
	James Wilkins	2	M			Va.		
358	Jno. B. Stewart	41	M	Farming		Va.		1
	Sarah Stewart	25	F			Va.		1
	Indianna Stewart	6	F			Va.		
	Mary F. Stewart	1	F			Va.		
375	Ro: Walls	30	M	Farming	75	Va.		1
	Mary Walls	26	F			Va.		
	Lauretta Walls	8	F			Va.		
	James Walls	6	M			Va.		
	Emiley Walls	4	F			Va.		
	Ro: Walls	2	M			Va.		
	Jos. Burnett	18	M	none		Va.		
377	James M. Hopkins	58	M	Wheelright	800	Va.		
	Ann E. Hopkins	43	F			Va.		
	Mary F. Hopkins	23	F			Va. blind		1
	Thos. Hopkins	19	M	Sailor		Va.		
	And: J. Hopkins	17	M	Sailor		Va.		
	Ann E. Hopkins	16	F			Va.		
379	Isaac Vaiden	58	M		1500	Va.		
	Judith Vaiden	58	F			Va.		
	Judith E. Vaiden	21	F			Va.		

No. of Family	Name	Age	Sex	Occupation	Value of Real Estate	Birth Place	Married within the Yr.	Over 20 & illiterate
	Lucy E. Vaiden	17	F			Va.		
	Vulosco Vaiden	14	M			Va.		
	James H. Allen	21	M	Schoolteacher		Va.		
	John B. Vaiden	16	M			Va.		
380	Thomas Lambeth	38	M	Farming		Va.		1
	Sarah Lambeth	30	F			Va.		
	George Lambeth	12	M			Va.		
	John Lambeth	9	M			Va.		
	Rosalie Lambeth	2	F			Va.		
381	John P. Turner	49	M	Minister, Bap.	5000	Va.		
	Louisa B. Turner	47	F			Va.		
	John D. Turner	16	M			Va.		
	Edmund P. Turner	15	M			Va.		
	Louisa K. Turner	7	F			Va.		
389	Seaton M. Cumber	38	M	Farming	400	Va.		1
	Ann Cumber	33	F			Va.		1
	Benj: Hix	31	M			Va.		1
	Henry Cumber	11	M			Va.		
	Isanna Cumber	9	F			Va.		
	Nelson Cumber	8	M			Va.		
	Benj: Cumber	7	M			Va.		
	Martha Cumber	4	F			Va.		
	Melville Cumber	2	M			Va.		
390	John Hix	19	M	Farming		Va.	1	
	Martha Hix	19	F			Va.	1	
391	Wm. Debriss	50	M	Shoemaker		Va.		
392	Martha Hazire(?)	23	F			Va.		1
	Larkin Harman	38	M	none		Va.		
	Susan Harman	29	F			Va.		1
	Wm. Harman	9	M			Va.		
	Turner Harman	6	M			Va.		
	Martha Harman	4	F			Va.		
	Leroy Harman	1(?)	M			Va.		
393	Richard Glazebrook	46	M	Farming		Va.		1
	Betsy Glazebrook	35	F			Va.		1
	Mary Glazebrook	6	F			Va.		
	Cynthia Glazebrook	5	F			Va.		
	Jas. Glazebrook	3	M			Va.		
394	Melville Vaiden	30	M	Farming	2000	Va.		
	Mary L. Vaiden	30	F			Va.		
	Aspesia Vaiden	6	F			Va.		
	Galba Vaiden	5	M			Va.		
	Albert H. Vaiden	4	M			Va.		
395	Ro: Drake	54(?)	M	Merchant	640	Va		
	Wm. Brake	18	M	Merchant		Va.		
	Armistead R. Manning	36(?)	M	none	300	Va.		
396	Chs. Roach	25	M	Lumber getting $30		Va.		
	Martha Roach	20	F			Va.		
	Wm. Roach	2	M			Va.		
398	Maria Blayton	50	F			Va.		
	Jno. H. Blayton	23	M	none		Va.		
	Mary T. Blayton	22	F			Va.		
	Maria W. Blayton	19	F			Va.		
	James S. Blayton	14	M			Va.		

Page 45

No. of Family	Name	Age	Sex	Occupation	Value of Real Estate	Birth-Place	Married within the Yr.	Over 20 & illiterate
399	Betsy Tyree	50	F			Va.		
	Patsy Tyree	40	F			Va.		
400	Sally Woodward	57	F			Va.		
	Micaj: Woodward	8	M			Va.		
	Wesley Woodward	11	M			Va.		
	Richd. Tyree	22	M	none		Va.		
401	Benj: Tyree	58	M	Farming		Va.		
	Nancy Tyree	40	F			Va.		1
	James Tyree	19	M	none		Va.		
	Wm. Tyree	16	M			Va.		
	George Tyree	13	M			Va.		
	Cyrus Tyree	11	M			Va.		
	Marion Tyree	9	F			Va.		
402	Ro: A. Saunders	27	M	Merchant		Va.		
	James S. Graves(?)	23	M	Merchant		Va.		
403	George Bradley	49	M	Farming	1300	Va.		
	Mary Stith	62	F			Va.		
	Nancy Bradley	39	F			Va.		
	Martha Bradley	16	F			Va.		
	Mary Bradley	15	F			Va.		
	Wm. Bradley	14	M			Va.		
	Maria L. Bradley	12	F			Va.		
	Ro: Bradley	10	M			Va.		
	Susan Bradley	9	F			Va.		
	Eliz: Bradley	7	F			Va.		
	Georgiana Bradley	6	F			Va.		
	Lutilda Bradley	3	F			Va.		
	Edward Bradley	9/12	M			Va.		
404	Elijah Ball	41	M	Merchant	3000	Va.		
	Martha A. Ball	36	F			Va.		
	Edmund Saunders	19	M			Va.		
	Lewellen Ball	13	M			Va.		
	Mary J. Ball	10	F			Va.		
	Betty W. Ball	9	F			Va.		
	Rebecca Ball	6	F			Va.		
	Wm. H. Ball	4	M			Va.		
	Ann M. Ball	2	F			Va.		
405	Sally H. Timberlake	50	F			Va.		
	Wm. Timberlake	35	M	Carpenter		Va.		
	Jane Timberlake	30	F			Va.		
	Martha Timberlake	25	F			Va.		
	Mary Timberlake	21	F			Va.		
	Warren Timberlake	20	M			Va.		
406	Jno. L. Merry	48	M	Farming		Va.		
407	Billy Burwell	58	M	Sawing		Va.		
408	Matilda Banks	35	F			Va.		
	Virginia Banks	10	F			Va.		
	Nat: Banks	8	M			Va.		
	Ro: Banks	5	M			Va.		
409	Tho: B. Sherman	54	M	Farming	20,000	Va.		
	Eliza D. Sherman	54	F			Va.		
	Henley B. Sherman	27	M	none		Va.		
	Tho, C. Winfree	27	M	Bricklayer		Va.		

Page 46

No. of Family	Name	Age	Sex	Occupation	Value of Real Estate	Birth place	Married within the Yr.	Over 20 & illiterate
410	James A. Smith	43	M	Farming	1000	Va.		
	John T. Smith	16	M			Va.		
	Wm. M. Smith	14	M			Va.		
411	Wm. B. Merry	54	M	Farming	1000	Va.		
	Ann Merry	55	F			Va.		
	Joice Merry	14	F			Va.		
412	Ro: L. Bowis	47	M	Farming		Va.		
	Cath: A. Bowis	44	F			Va.		
	Wm. A. Bowis	11	M			Va.		
	Mary E. Bowis	10	F			Va.		
	Stanhope, M. Bowis	6	M			Va.		
	Jno: R. Bowis	2	M			Va.		
412	Edmund Richardson	75	M	Farming	1000	Va.		
	Daniel O. Atkinson	33	M	Cabinate Maker		Va.		
	Eliz: F. Atkinson	27	F			Va.		
	James A. Richardson	8	M			Va.		
	Susan A. Atkinson	6	F			Va.		
	Wm. E. Atkinson	5	M			Va.		
	Geo. A. Atkinson	3	M			Va.		
414	Mary Thompson	37	F			Va. pauper		
	Mary F. Thompson	11	F			Va.		
	Rebecca W. Thompson	10	F			Va.		
	Ann E. Thompson	7	F			Va.		
	Jno: H. Thompson	6	M			Va.		
	Isaac Howle	30	M	none		Va.		
416	Wm. A. Green	44	M	Farming		Va.		
	Eliz: Green	74	F		600	Va.		
	Maria D. Green	49	F			Va.		
	Gid: D. Wade	30	M	Farming		Va.	1	
	Betty C. Wade	21	F			Va.	1	
417	Mary Howle	46	F			Va.		1
	Mary Howle	18	F			Va.		
	Geo. W. Howle	17	M	none		Va.		
	Henry I. Howle	15	M			Va.		
	John Crabbin	25	M			Va.		
418	James Ladd	64	M	Farming		Va.		
420	Miles C. Crowdir	55	M	Farming	400	Va.		
	Sarah M. Crowdir	49	F			Va.		1
	John D. Crowdir	21	M	none		Va.		
	Maria L. Crowdir	17	F			Va.		
	Sarah C. Crowdir	14	F			Va.		
	Miles C. Crowdir	7	M			Va.		
	Martha F. Crowdir	3	F			Va.		
421	Wm Ford	64	M	Farming		Va.		1
	Fleming Adams	34	M	none		Va.		1
	Lucy A. Ford	32	F			Va.		
	Mary Ford	18	F			Va.		
424	Betsy Pomfrey	50	F			Va.		1
	Nancy Kent	29	F			Va.		1
	Betsy Kent	6	F			Va.		
425	Jno: Houching	52	M	Bricklayer		Va.		
	Eliz: Houching	44	F			Va.		
	Andrew Houching	24	M	Shoemaker		Va.		

No. of Family	Name	Age	Sex	Occupation	Value of Real Estate	Birth place	Married within the Yr.	Over 20 & illiterate
	Benj: F. Houching	21	M	none		Va.		
	Silas Houching	14	M			Va.		
	Sarah A. Houching	12	S			Va.		
	Jno: Houching	5	M			Va.		
426	Leonard C. Crump	30	M	Farming	4000	Va.		
	Emiley A. Crump	21	F			Va.		
	Sallie B. Crump	1	F			Va.		
	Collier C. Frayser	15	M			Va.		
427	Charles C. Crump	46	M	Farming	3000	Va.		
	Thomas Goodman	23	M	none		Va.		
428	Ro: Crump	23	M	Farming	2500	Va.		
430	Augustine Crump	31	M	Physician	5000	Va.	1	
	Mary C. Crump	25	F			Va.	1	
	George P. Crump	61	M	none		Va.		
	E.G. Crump	43	M	Lawyer		Va.		
	Wm. R. Clarke	21	M			Va.		
432	George Benn	47	M	Carpenter	300	Va.		
	Amanda Benn	18	F			Va.		
	George Benn	15	M			Va.		
	Thos: Benn	13	M			Va.		
	Junius Benn	11	M			Va.		
	Ann Benn	7	F			Va.		
	Emeline Benn	6	F			Va.		
434	J.L. Poindexter	54	M	Farming	10000	Va.		
	Martha C. Poindexter	52	F			Va.		
	M.A. Poindexter	22	F			Va.		
	J.L. Poindexter, Jr.	15	M			Va.		
	M.E. Poindexter	10	F			Va.		
435	Jno: C. Apperson	50	M	Farming		Va.		
	Susan T. Apperson	38	F			Va.		
	Mary Poindexter	73	F			Va.		
	Fanny P. Perkins	50	F			Va.		
	Susan A. Armistead	65	F			Va.		
	Willianna Armistead	37	F			Va.		
	Ro: C. Apperson	17	M			Va.		
	Jno: C. Apperson	15	M			Va.		
	Wm. A. Apperson	12	M			Va.		
	Sam'l H. Apperson	9	M			Va.		
	Mary E. Apperson	6	F			Va.		
	Edward W. Apperson	3	M			Va.		
	Susan M. Apperson	6/12	F			Va.		
436	Jesse Crabbin	47	M	Farming		Va.		1
	Eliz: Crabbin	29	F			Va.		1
	Warren Ross	23	M			Va.		1 bl
	Emiley Crabbin	10	F			Va.		
	Dyonesia Crabbin	8	F			Va.		
	Sally Crabbin	1	F			Va.		
437	John Pearman	32	M	Blacksmith	200	Va.		
	Dan: Patterson	16	M	Blacksmith		Va.		
438	Hugh Williams	33	M	Carpenter		Wales	1	1
	Harriet Williams	21	F			Va.	1	
439	Jasper A. Clayton	37	M	Farming	50	Va.		
	Fanny C. Clayton	64	F		2800	Va.		
	Eliza T. Clayton	28	F			Va.		

Page 47

No. of Family	Name	Age	Sex	Occupation	Value of Real Estate	Birth Place	Married within the Yr.	Over 20 & illiterate
	Wyatt H. Clayton	45	M	none		Va.		
	Jasper A. Clayton, Jr	7/12	M			Va.		
	Wm. B. Clayton	13	M			Va.		
442	Martha W. Bathins	34	F			Va.		
	Ro: B. Bathins	8	M			Va.		
	Martha J. Bathins	6	F			Va.		
443	John G. Howle	20	M	Farming		Va.		
444	James F. Gerry	34	M	Carpenter		Va.		
	Susanna F. Gary	28	F			Va.		
	Edwin J. Gary	10	M			Va.		
	Mary E. Gary	7	F			Va.		
	Servatus W. Gary	6	M			Va.		
	Theo: I. Gary	4	M			Va.		
	Jno: F. Gary	3/12	M			Va.		
	Rebecca Gary	3/12	F			Va.		
445	Albert T. Perkinson	39	M	Farming	3500	Va.		
	Eliz: C. Christian	57	F			Va.		
	Ann E. Perkinson	28	F			Va.		
	Maria L. Christian	24	F			Va.		
	Jordan C. Parkinson	10	M			Va.		
	Edmonia C. Parkinson	8	F			Va.		
	Ann E. Parkinson	6	F			Va.		
	Jno: F. Parkinson	23	M			Va.		
	Joshua Parkinson	1	M			Va.		
446	Gilson Bathins, Agt.	25	M	Farming	1000	Va.		1
447	Ro: Dennett	58	M	Farming	150	Va.		
448	Ro: F. Gary	25	M	Farming		Va.		
	Cath: Wright	27	F			Va.		
	Ro: Bathins	21	M	Farming		Va.		1
	Mary T. Wright	6	F			Va.		
	Thomas Wright	4	M			Va.		
449	Jno: F. Christian	58	M	Physician		Va.		
	Ann Christian	80	F			Va.		
	Sam'l P. Christian	29	M	Physician	5285	Va.		
	Amelia C. Christian	21	F			Va.		
450	Meriwether Lewis	52	M	Farming	300	Va.		
	Pamelia Lewis	35	F			Va.		
	Ro: R. Lewis	16	M			Va.		
	Wm. A. Lewis	13	M			Va.		
	Ann E. Lewis	11	F			Va.		
	Martha T. Lewis	9	F			Va.		
	Mary E. Lewis	8	F			Va.		
452	John Crabbin	54	M	Farming	300	Va.		1
	Lucy Crabbin	28	F			Va.		
	James Crabbin	22	M			Va.		1
	Thos: Crabbin	19	M			Va.		
	Susan Crabbin	15	F			Va.		
	Ann Crabbin	5	F			Va.		
454	Francis Nelson	41	M	Farming	40	Va.		
	Latitia R. Nelson	32	F			Va.		
	Sally B. Nelson	11	F			Va.		
	Philip M. Nelson	6	M			Va.		
	Lucy G. Nelson	4	F			Va.		
	Wm. P. Nelson	1	M			Va.		

Page 49

No. of Family	Name	Age.	Sex	Occupation.	Value of Real Estate	Birth place.	Married within the Yr.	Over 20 & illiterate
455	Walter P. Hogan	26	M	Farming		Va.		
456	Thos: W. Atkinson	56	M	Farming	500	Va.		
	Mary Glenn?	87	F			Va.		
	Sarah Sansum?	51	F			Va.		
	Wm. V. Atkinson	14	M			Va.		
457	Jno. R. Dixon	29	M	Farming		Va.		1
	Mary A. Dixon	33	F			Va.		
	Julius Dixon	7	M			Va.		
	Jane S. Dixon	5	F			Va.		
	Eliz: Dixon	3	F			Va.		
	James Dixon	1	M			Va.		
458	Thos: S. Dixon	32	M	Farming		Va.		1
	Eliza A. Dixon	21	F			Va.		
	Wm. P. Jennings	20	M	none		Va.		
	Eliz. Dixon	3	F			Va.		
	Wm. J. Dixon	1	M			Va.		
459	James H. Lipscomb	21	M	Merchant		Va.		
	Nelson Muse	16	M	Merchant		Va.		
460	Henry Toler	43	M	Farming		Va.		
	Susan Toler	46	F		9000	Va.		
	Henrietta Toler	6	F			Va.		
461	Wm. C. Cooke	32	M	Farming	1000	Va.		
	Octavia R. Cooke	20	F			Va.		
	Richad: D. Cooke	3	M			Va.		
	Alice A. Cooke	5/12	F			Va.		
	Wm. H. Vaughan	19	M	wheelright		Va.		
462	William Vaughan	61	M	farming		Va.		
	Henry W. Vaughan	27	M	none		Va.		
	John M. Vaughan	15	M			Va.		
463	A. G. Jones	28	M	Physician		Va.		
464	Wm. T. Walls	36	M	merchant	700	Va.		
	Martha A. E. Walls	28	F			Va.		
	Wm. P. Davis	22	M	none		Va.		
	Wm. B. Crabbin	24	M	none		Va.		
	Wm P. Ross	23	M	none		Va.		1
	Victoria Walls	2	F			Va.		
465	Geo. P. Bailey	44	M	farming	2500	Va.		
	Ann E. Bailey	44	F			Va.		
	Sally P. Bailey	19	F			Va.		
	Mary F. Bailey	17	F			Va.		
	Ann E. Bailey	10	F			Va.		
	Letitia Bailey	7	F			Va.		
466	Judith Crabbin	60	F			Va.		
	Cath: Johnson	60	F			Va.		
468	Theo: A. Lacy	47	M	Farming	3500	Va.		
	Ann E. Lacy	29	F			Va.		
	S. O. Lacy	13	F			Va.		
	Theo: S. Lacy	7	M			Va.		
	Arch: E. Lacy	3	M			Va.		
	Nora B. Lacy	1	F			Va.		
469	Thos. S. Morris, Jr	33	M	Farming	1500	Va.		
	Nancy Lightfoot	60	F			Va.		
	Wm. Lightfoot	25?	M	none		Va.		
	Lucy A. Morris	30	F			Va.		

Page 50

No. of Family	Name	Age	Sex	Occupation	Value of Real Estate	Birthplace	Married within the Yr.	Over 20 & illiterate
	Lucy L. Morris	5	F			Va.		
	Florence E. Morris	2	F			Va		
470	Thomas Timberlake	48	M	Merchant	1200	Va.		
	Mary T. Timberlake	44	F			Va.		
	Th: N. Timberlake, Jr.	18	M-			Va.		
	Maria L. Timberlake	10	F			Va.		
	Harriet A. Timberlake	14	F			Va.		
	Jno: T. Timberlake	12	M			Va.		
	Frances Timberlake	8	F			Va.		
	Jas. P. Timberlake	6	M			Va.		
	Jno. Timberlake	51	M	Merchant		Va.		
471	Isaac Jennings	40	M	Farming	500	Va.		
	Martha Jennings	26	F			Va.		
	Barshe Woodward	50	F			Va.		1
	Wm. Jennings	13	M			Va.		
	Mary J. Jennings	11	F			Va.		
	Adias Jennings	8	F			Va.		
	Isaac S. Jennings	6	M			Va.		
	O.S.T. Jennings	1	M			Va.		
472	John C. Martin	35	M	Farming	250	Va.		
	Frances Martin	20	F			Va.		
	James B. Martin	1	M			Va.		
473	James Vaiden	40	M	Farming	3990	Va.		
474	John Parke	58	M	Physician		Va.		
475	Richard S. Eggleston	35	M	Farming	300	Va.		
476	James Stamper	50	M	Farming	3600	Va.		
	Martha J. Stamper	27	F			Va.		
	Octavia E. Stamper	14	F			Va.		
	James Stamper, Jr.	3	M			Va.		
	John Stamper	1	M			Va.		
	Mary F. Sansenn?	25	F			Va.		
479	John Wright	57	M	Farming	800	Va.		
	Martha A. Wright	57	F			Va.		
	Wm. D. Wright	29	M	Farming		Va.		
	Sarah Wright	20	F			Va.		
	Joseph Wright	23	M	Carpenter		Va.		
	Martha J. Wright	7/12	F			Va.		
480	Mitchell W. Bradley	54	M	Farming	4500	Va.		
481	Saml. C. Taylor	51	M	Farming	600	Va.		
	Martha Gathright	68	F			Va.		
	Orina Taylor	37	F			Va.		
	Martha A. Howle	23	F			Va.		
	James T. Taylor	14	M			Va.		
	Littleberry W. Taylor	12	M			Va.		
	Edw. H. Taylor	10	M			Va.		
	Saml. T. Taylor	8	M			Va.		
	Geo. W. Taylor	4	M			Va.		
	Zachary Taylor	1	M			Va.		
482	Barthol: Lacy	47	M	Carpenter		Va.		
	Rich: B. Lacy	20	M	none		Va.		
	Mary A. Lacy	16	F			Va.		
	John C. Lacy	14	M			Va.		
	Eliza E. Lacy	12	F			Va.		
	Geo. R. Lacy	10	M			Va.		

Page 51

No. of Family	Name	Age	Sex	Occupation	Value of Real Estate	Birthplace	Married within the Yr.	Over 20 & illiterate
483	Anslem ? Bailey	75	M	Farming		Va.		
	Martha Bailey	67	F			Va.		
	Martha F. Bailey	24	F			Va.		
	Ballard D. Bailey	22	M	none		Va.		
	Mary W. Bailey	19	F			Va.		
484	Charles Binns	72	M	Farming	4500	Va.		
	Chs: H. Binns	38	M	Farming		Va.		
	Adelaide B. Binns	28	F			Va.		
	Martha E. Binns	14	F			Alabama		
	Amelia A. Binns	9	F			Alabama		
	Chas. H. Binns, Jr	7	M			Va.		
	Wm. E. Binns	4	M			Va.		
	Mary C. Binns	3	F			Va.		
485	John G. Carter	40	M	Physician	4000	Va.		
	Maria Southall	62	F			Va.		
	Lutilda L. Carter	40	F			Va.		
	Ann E. Bathins	25	F			Va.		
	Lutilda L. Carter	12	F			Va.		
	Margaret A. Carter	10	F			Va.		
	John G. Carter, Jr.	5	M			Va.		
486	Ro: Batkins	52	M	Overseer		Va.		1
	Susan V. Bathins	14	F			Va.		
487	John H. Christian	28	M	Farming	1500	Va.		
	Martha M. Christian	24	F			Va.		
	Mary S. Clopton	24	F			Va.		
	Lucy Christian	3	F			Va.		
	James C. Christian	7/12	M			Va.		
488	Richard D. Carter	24	M	Farming	3000	Va.		
	Maria L. Carter	23	F			Va.		
	Lucy L. Bradley	21	F			Va.		
	Mary L. Bradley	16	F			Va.		
	Anne M. Bradley	14	F			Va.		
489	James W. Talley	34	M	Farming		Va.		
490	Mary B. Price	60	F			Va.		
	Betty S. Price	27	F			Va.		
	Lurina P. Price	19	F			Va.		
	Jno. W. Royster	24	M	Physician		Va.	1	
	Lucy C. Royster	25	F			Va.	1	
491	Caroline Tyler	47	F			Va.		1
	Hezekiah Tyler	16	M	none		Va.		
493	Geo. W. Taylor	31	M	farming	928	Va.		
	Martha A. Taylor	20	F			Va.		
	Ann E. Taylor	24	F			Va.		
	Mary E. Taylor	2	F			Va.		
494	Henry M. Sherman	47	M	Farming	6600	Va.		
	Prudence Primrose	50	F			Va.		1
	B. A. Curtis	24	M	Schoolteacher		Va.		
	Michael Sherman	14	M			Va.		
	Sarah V. Sherman	10	F			Va.		
495	Nancy Bailey	73	F			Va.		1
496	Geo. W. Warren	52	M	Shoemaker		Va.		
	Eliz: G. Warren	49	F			Va.		
	Eliza. M. Warren	23	F			Va.		
	Nancy C. Warren	21	F			Va.		

Page 52

No. of Family.	Name.	Age	Sex	Occupation	Value of Real Estate	Birth Place.	Married within the Yr.	Over 20 & Illiterate.
	Jno. H. Warren	19	M	Farming		Va.		
	Sarah J. Warren	17	F			Va.		
	Eliz: E. Warren	12	F			Va.		
497	Chs: G.Pearson	28	M	Farming	$1500-	Va.		
	Sarah E.Pearson	34	F			Va.		
	Wm.E.Christian	30	M	None	3600	Va.	1	
	Ann.E.Christian	20	F			Va.	1	
	Wm.G.Pearson	1	M			Va.		
	Lucy C.Pearson	2/12	F			Va.		
498	Caroline M.Christian	56	F		4500	Va.		
	Sarah A.Christian	33	F			Va.		
	Edmd.F.Christian	25	M	Farming		Va.		
	Henry B.Christian	19	M	None		Va.		
	Jones,R.Christian	16	M			Va.		
	Betty I.Christian	10	F			Va.		
	Eugenia Christian	7	F			Va.		
	William C.Christian	5	M			Va.		
499	Chris:S.Christian	45	F		12,000	Va.		
	Edmd.Christian	24	M	Physician		Va.	1	
	Mary M.Christian	22	F			Va.		
	Elizabeth Christian	21	F			Va.	1	
	Robert Christian	14	M			Va.		
	Christiana Christian	7	F			Va.		
500	Vernon Mountcastle	21	M	Overseer		Va.		
	James E.Binns,	22	M	Miller		Va.		
501	Wm R.C.Douglas	40	M	Farming	10,000	Va.		
	Lucy A.Douglas	37	F			Va.		
	Wm. Walter Douglas	16	M			Va.		
	Henry T.Douglas	12	M			Va.		
	Eliz.Joan Douglas	10	F			Va.		
	Mary Douglas	8	F			Va.		
	Lucy A.Douglas	5	F			Va.		
	John B.Douglas	1	M			Va.		
502	Miles Tucker	23	M	Overseer		Va.		
503	John P.Anderson	66	M	Overseer		Va.		
	Ann Anderson	52	F			Va.		
504	Richard Morriss	43	M	Farming		Va.		1
	Agness Morriss	36	F			Va.		1
	Wm.Henry Morriss	15	M			Va.		
	Irena Morriss	13	F			Va.		
	Tho; J.Morriss	9	M			Va.		
	Richd.Morriss,Jr	6	M			Va.		
	Betty T.Morriss	1	F			Va.		
505	Geo: W.Poindexter	52	M	Farming	400	Va.		
	Agnes,C.Poindexter	37	F			Va.		
	Susan W.Poindexter	18	F			Va.		
	Willis L.Poindexter	10	M			Va.		
	Edwin P Poindexter	8	M			Va.		
	Mary E.Poindexter	6	F			Va.		
	Lafayett W.Poindexter	4	M			Va.		
	Frances P.Poindexter	1	F			Va.		
506	Philn: Woodward	55	M	Farming	150	Va.		1
	Cath: Woodward	45	F			Va.		1
	Nancy J.Woodward	12	F			Va.		
	Susan Woodward	8	F			Va.		

Page 53

No of Family	Name	Age	Sex	Occupation	Value of Real Estate	Birth Place	Married within the Yr.	Over 20 & Illiterate
	Geo: P.Woodward	6	M			Va.		
507	Tempey Bailey	80	F			Va. pauper		
	John Mullen	17	M	None		Va.		
509	Herman Chandler	56	M	Farming	$1200	Va.		
	Edwd. Chandler	12	M			Va.		
510	Wm. Bond	33	M	Farming		Va.		1
	Mary Bond	32	F			Va.		1
	Emily Bond	11	F			Va.		
	Martha Bond	9	F			Va.		
	Mary C. Bond	6	F			Va.		
	Eliz: Bond	2	F			Va.		
511	Wm. L. Dennett	41	M	Farming		Va.		
	Sarah Dennett	45	F			Va.		
	James Dennett	12	M			Va.		
	Chs. Dennett	10	M			Va.		
512	Mary F. Tucker	38	F			Va.	Pauper	
	Martha C. Tucker	12	F			Va.	"	
	James D. Tucker	12	M			Va.	"	
	Sarah J. Tucker	10	F			Va.	"	
513	Cath: Pomfrey	52	F			Va.		
	William Turner	21	M			Va.		
	James P. Pomfrey	12	M			Va.		
514	Benj; P. Apperson	57	M	Farming	$150	Va.	1	
	Eliz: Apperson	35	F			Va.	1	1
515	Fleming Oakley	48	M	none		Va.		1 p
	Susan Oakley	42	F			Va.		1 p
	James A. Oakley	16	M	none		Va.		p
	Wm T. Oakley	22	M	None		Va.		1
	Louisa Oakley	9	F			Va.		
	Martha Oakley	5	F			Va.		
517	Ann M. Meanley	48	F			Va.		
	Maria L. Meanley	20	F			Va.		
	Sarah H. Meanley	18	F			Va.		
	Cordelia W. Meanley	14	F			Va.		
	Martha L. Meanley	12	F			Va.		
	John P. Meanley	10	M			Va.		
	Geo: M. Meanley	8	M			Va.		
518	Alex: Proovo ?	29	M	Carpenter		Va.		
	Margaret Proovo	22	F			Va.		
	Ann A. Proovo	2	F			Va.		
	Martha Clarke	18	F			Va.		
520	Mildred Dunn	50	F		$400	Va.		1
	Mildred A. Dunn	22	F			Va.		
521	William P Richardson	33		Physician		Va.		
	Eliz: A. Richardson	28	F			Va.		
522	John Slater	55	M	Farming	$10,975	Va.		
	Fluvanna P. Slater	47	F			Va.		
	John S. Slater	24	M	Merchant	500	Va.	1	
	Virginia. W. Slater	19	F			Va.		
	Leonard A. Slater	14	M			Va.		
	Ellen B. Slater	8	F			Va.		
	Emiley W. Slater	5	F			Va.		
	James M. Dillard	23	M	Merchant		Va.		

No of Family	Name	Age	Sex	Occupation	Value of Real Estate	Birth Place	Married within the Yr.	Over 20 & Illiterate
523	Fleming Mills	20	M	Farming		Va.		
524	Beverley Crump	39	M	Farming	734	Va.		
	Oliver M. Chandler	29	M	Farming		Va.		
	John B. Dandridge	31	M	None		Va.		
Tavern:	Ann L. Crump	27	F			Va.		
	Margaret H. Crump	5	F			Va.		
	Eliz: P. Crump	2	F			Va.		
	Mathew J. Harden	21	M	Mail carrier		Va.		
525	Thomas Barkam	29	M	Constable	50	Va.		
	John P. Pierce	27	M	Lawyer	50	Va.		
526	Jail: Martha Ellyson	70	F		1000	Va.		Debt.
527	James M. Bradley	35	M	Merchant		Va.	1	
	Mary E. Bradley	24	F			Va.	1	
	Richd. E. Frayser	20	M	Merchant		Va.		
528	Betty W. Stark	47	F		500	Va.		
	P. C. Watkins	70	F			Va.		
529	Geo: Williamson	48	M	Physician	500	Va.		
	Maria Wilkinson	57	F			Va.		
	Mary A. Williamson	30	F			Va.		
530	Isaac Vaiden	55	M	Farming		Va.		
	Caroline Vaiden	45	F			Va.		
	Wm. H Vaiden	25	M	Carpenter		Va.		
	Eliz: Hockaday	19	F			Va.		
	Juliet Hockaday	14	F			Va.		
	Mary E. Vaiden	11	F			Va.		
	Cynthia M. Vaiden	9	F			Va.		
	Susan C. Vaiden	8	F			Va.		
	Isaac H. Vaiden	5	M			Va.		
531	Richard T. Lacy	50	M	Lawyer	11,000	Va.		
	Ellen G. Lacy	35	F			Va.		
	Sally E. Lacy	13	F			Va.		
	Benj: W. Lacy	11	M			Va.		
	Ellen G. Lacy	10	F			Va.		
	Richmond T. Lacy	8	M			Va.		
	Betty W. Lacy	5	F			Va.		
	Lane? Lacy	4	M			Va.		
	Thos: H. Lacy	2	M			Va.		
	Isabella Robertson	24	F			New York		
532	Sam Binns	50	M			Va.		1
	Martha Tucker	40	F			Va		
	Archer Tucker	14	M			Va.		
	Ann E. Tucker	12	F			Va.		
	Richd. Tucker	10	M			Va.		
	Miles Tucker	8	M			Va.		
	Martha Tucker	6	F			Va.		
533	James Chandler	41	M	Farming	1250	Va.		
	Mary Chandler	30	F			Va.		
	Susan E. Chandler	11	F			Va.		
	Hester Chandler	5	F			Va.		
	Emma Chandler	3	F			Va.		
	Wm H. Chandler	1	M			Va		
534	Isaac Otey	63	M	Farming	1450	Va.		
	Betty Otey	24	F			Va.		
	Martha Otey	21	F			Va.		

Page 55

No. of Family	Name	Age	Sex	Occupation	Value of Real Estate	Birth place	Married within the Yr.	Over 20 & Illiterate
535	Thos: H. Terrell	60	M	Farming	3952	Va.		
	Ann H. Terrell	23	F			Va.		
	Geo: P. Terrell	17	M	None		Va.		
	Leigh R. Terrell	15	M			Va.		
	Arthur C. Terrell	11	M			Va.		
536	Major A. Pomfrey	40	M	Farming	285	Va.		
	Elvira Pomfrey	74	F			Va.		
Poor-	Margaret A. Pomfrey	31	F			Va.		
	Frances E. Pomfrey	9	F			Va.		
	Wm. A. Pomfrey	7	M			Va.		
	Geo: M. Pomfrey	5	M			Va.		
house	Ann E. Pomfrey	3	F			Va.		
	Mery Pomfrey	2	F			Va.		
	Isaac Howle	60	M	none		Va.	Pauper	1
	Dandridge Martin	80	M	none		Va.	Pauper	1
	Polly Clarke	51	F			Va.	Pauper	1
	Richard Barker	18	M	None		Va.	Pauper	
	William Hill	13	M			Va.	pauper	
	John Martin	7	M			Va.	pauper	
537	Julius Martin	68	M	Farming	750	Va.		
	Eliza Martin	25	F			Va.		1
	Jno: B. Williams,	12	M			Va.		
538	Jno: Warner	34	M	Farming	1000	Va.		
	Ann. Warner	33	F			Va.		
	James Warner	8	M			Va.		
	Louisiana Warner	5	F			Va.		
539	Ro: Howle	40	M	Farming	3225	Va.	1	
	Mary H. Howle	26	F			Va.	1	
	Major D. Apperson	53	M	None		Va.		
540	Abner Mitchell	60	M	Farming		Va.		
	Susan M. Mitchell	49	F			Va.		
	James R. Mitchell	23	M	Carpenter		Va.		
	John R. Mitchell	18	M	Merchant		Va.		
	Joice P. Mitchell	16	F			Va.		
	Lucius E. Mitchell	10	M			Va.		
541	John D. Christian	50	M	Clerk of Court	7000	Va.		
	Octavia St. C. Christian	41	F			Va.		
	Bat: D. Christian	22	M	Asst. Marshall		Va.		
	James Christian	21	M	Constable		Va.		
	John D. Christian	18	M	Farming		Va.		
	William Christian	15	M			Va.		
	James S. Christian	13	M			Va.		
	Armistead Christian	8	M			Va.		
	Octavia St. C. Christian	6	F			Va.		
	Augustine Christian	1	M			Va.		
542	Wm. P. Waring	38	M	Farming	6000	Va.		
	Maria E. Waring	26	F			Va.		
	Wm. H. Waring	8	M			Va.		
	Mary E. L. Waring	9	F			Va.		
	Thos: B. Waring	6	M			Va.		
	Payne Waring	4	M			Va.		
	Jno W. Waring	2	M			Va.		
	John Madison	22	M	Farming		Va.		
	Ro: L. Waring	8/12	M			Va.		

Page 56

No. of Family	Name.	Age	Sex	Occupation	Value of Real Estate	Birthplace	Married within the Yr.	Over 20 & Illiterate
545	Kitty Binns	40	F			Va.		1 p.
	Sam Binns	8	M			Va.	Pauper d&d	
	Isaac Binns	7	M			Va.	Pauper d&d	
	Susan Binns	28	F			Va.	"	1
	Washington Binns	8	M			Va.	"	
	Mary Jane Binns	6	F			Va.	"	
	Geo: Binns	5/12	M			Va.		
546	James Howle	32	M	None		Va.		1

```
Total number of dwellings. . . . . . . . . . . . . . . . . . 535
Total white males. . . . . . . . . . . . . . . . . . . . . . 1111
Total White females. . . . . . . . . . . . . . . . . . . . . 1110
Total number of white inhabitants. . . . . . . . . . . . . . 2221

Colored males. . . . . . . . . . . . . . . . . . . . . . . . 198
Colored females. . . . . . . . . . . . . . . . . . . . . . . 235
Total number of free colored inhabitants. . . . . . . . . .  433

Total free population, both white & colored. . . . . . . .  2654
```

ABSTRACTS OF THE APPLICATION PAPERS OF REVOLUTIONARY PENSIONERS
OF NEW KENT COUNTY, VA.

JOHN BROWN, 2nd. (File No. S. 39,319; certificate no. 4732.) May 15, 1818, when he was 55 years of age John Brown, 2nd., of New Kent County, Va., made affidavit in open court that he enlisted in James City Co., Va., in May 1778 as a private in Colo. Porterfield's regt., and served to the end of the war. He was in the battle when Gates was defeated, and received his discharge at Little York, Va.

The signatures of the presiding judges of New Kent County Court appear on this paper and are: Robert Warren, Robert Graves, Seaton W. Crump, Wm Douglas and Beverly Crump. Bartholomew Dandridge signed as Clerk of Ct.

The pension of $8 per month was granted Oct. 21, 1818 commencing May 15, 1818. This was dropped Nov. 26 1819 upon information that Colo. Porterfield's was a State Regt. and not Continental.

March 15, 1808 John Brown, 2nd. had received a Military Bounty Land Warrant for 200 acres as private in Continental Line. This was signed by Wm. Price, Reg. of Land Office.

RICHARD BAKER. (File No. R. 412; certificate No. 3240.) Nov. 13, 1818, when he was 58 yrs. of age Richard Baker made affidavit in New Kent County Court before the presiding judges, stating that he now lives in Henrico County, but in 1778 when a resident of New Kent Co., he enlisted in the Continental Forces of the Rev. War in Capt. Bentley's Co., of 1st, Va. Regt. He was in the battles of Guilford, Cambden, at the siege of Little York, and was discharged near Charleston, South Carolina.

The signatures of the judges of the court appear on this paper and are: Robert Christian, John H. Christian, Beverly Crump and John H. Webb. Bartholomew Dandridge signs as Clerk of New Kent County.

A pension of $8. per month was granted Feb. 10- 1819.

July 4, 1836 Frances Baker, widow of Richard Baker makes affidavit in the court of Henrico County, Va., stating that she is 67 years of age and that Richard Baker died Dec. 3, 1827, leaving 2 children; a son Richard of lawful age and a daughter Elizabeth who was under the age of 16 when her father died. She, Frances, was married to Richard Baker in July 1810. This affidavit is signed by Wm Richardson, Justice of the Peace of Henrico Co.

Frances Baker's claim was denied. (Because they were married after Jan. 1st, 1794, the date mentioned in the Act allowing widows' pensions.)

JOHN BREEDING. (File no. S. 17, 862; certificate no. 23708.) March 17, 1834, John Breeding makes affidavit in New Kent County Court before the presiding judges and states that he is 75 years of age and is a resident of New Kent County, Va. In 1781 he entered the service of the U.S. as a militiaman under Capt. George Baker of that county, in the regiment of Colo. Richmond Allen and served 3 months. He was stationed at Williamsburg and Yorktown. He served another 3 mos. enlistment in the Company of Capt. John Bacon of New Kent County, and was again sent to Williamsburg. He served a third enlistment of 3 mos. in the company of Capt. Baker again. He was discharged a short time before the Siege of Yorktown. He served under Gen. Nelson and Maj. Ragsdale. He was born in New Kent Co. in 1757 and has always lived there.

The signatures of the judges presiding on that date are: Wm. H. Macon, Beverly Crump, Robert Graves, Jno. A. Taylor and Thomas H. Terrell.

A pension was granted for 9 months service as a private.

ANSALEM BAILEY. (File no. S. 37,702; certificate No.) July 9, 1818, Ansalem Bailey makes affidavit before the presiding judges of the Court of New Kent County, stating that he is 58 yrs. old and has been living in Hanover Co., Va., for the past three years, but prior to that he had always lived in New Kent Co., therefore it was as a resident of New Kent Co., that he enlisted in the Rev. War as a private in the Infantry Co., of Capt. Abner Crump of New Kent Co., in Colo. George Gibson's Regt. of Va. Line, for 3 yrs. service. He served his full term and was discharged at Philadelphia, Pa. He was in the battles of Monmouth, Stoney Point, Fowler's Hook and White Marsh where he was taken prisoner with several other Americans. Mostly through his planning they made their escape and joined their Gen.(Muhlenburg) at Valley Forge. He received a wound in the calf of the leg at Monmouth. He was also at Yorktown during the siege by the united armies of France and America.

The signatures of the judges who presided at New Kent Co., Court that day appear on this paper and are: John H. Christian, John L. Poindexter, Jno. S. Webb and Wm. Douglas.

A pension of $96. a year was granted Mch. 22, 1819, but was stopped under Act of May 1820.

In June 1820 this soldier made a new application for pension; again appeared in the Court of New Kent County and affirmed that his service had been in the Continental Line. At this date he was 62 yrs. of age and said he had a wife, Susannah Bailey aged 28 yrs., and 3 children viz: Rebecca aged 6, Martha aged 4 and Ansalem aged 1 yr. and a free boy aged 16, Bailey stated at this appearance that he enlisted Nov. 21, 1776 and served until Dec. 22, 1779.

Mathew Higgins and Parks Martin, freeholders of the said county were directed to appraise Bailey's property, which was as follows: 1 grey mare at $10, bay colt $25, 1 heifer $5, cow & calf $15, 13 hogs of different sizes $20, 1 cart & plough $10; total $95.75.

The judges of New Kent Court signing at this date were: Robert Graves, Robert Christian, Jno. H. Christian and John L. Poindexter.

The pension was restored.

In 1830 Ansalem Bailey again applied for a pension stating that he had lost his certificate. This application was drawn in Hanover Co., Va. before Judge Ed. B. Crenshaw. Bailey then said he was 70 years old and had a wife and 7 small children.

The affidavit of Peter Francisco of Buckingham Co., Va., (then Sergt. at Arms of the House of Delegates) states that he and Ansalem Bailey were comrades at Stoney Point, Monmouth and Mud Island and that Bailey was a good and brave soldier.

The affidavit of Capt. Peter Foster also is attached, and states that he and Bailey were together in several engagements and he well knew they were serving in the Continental Line. This paper also was drawn before Judge Ed. B. Crenshaw of Hanover Co., Va.

The affidavit of J. Marshall states he is sure Bailey served in the war although they were not together in the army.

Capt. A. V. Crump signed a voucher stating Ansalem Bailey was in his Co., of 1st, Va. Regt.; enlisted 21 Nov. 1776 and served until 22 Dec. 1779.

Rev. John B. Clopton and Carrell Fleming Chappell testified that Bailey then lived in their neighborhood and was truthful.

A letter filed with these papers and dated 1. 12, 1830 and signed by J. H. Eaton (Secy. of War) says: An Act passed Oct. 1777 by the State of Virginia discloses that "Col. George Gibson's Regt. shall be placed on Continental establishment in lieu of the 9th Regt. which was captured at Germantown.

Wm. H. Richardson, a notary public of City of Richmond, Va. certified a paper for Ansalem Bailey and it was witnessed by J. W. Pleasants, May 20, 1830.

REVOLUTIONARY PENSIONERS.   Page 59

BENJAMIN CHAPPELL. (File No. S. 38, 599; certificate No. 8006.) July 9, 1818, Benj. Chappell made affidavit before the judges of New Kent Co., Court that he was 62 years of age and a resident of New Kent Co., and had enlisted from that county in the Rev. War as a private in the Co., of Capt. John Fleming and Colo. Richard Parker's 1st Va. Regt. of Continental establishment at Williamsburg in Aug. 1776, for 3 years service; served his term and was discharged at Stoney Point, N. Y. He was in battles of Brandywine, Germantown, Monmouth and Mud Island Fort.

The signatures of the judges presiding on that day were: John H. Christian, John L. Poindexter, John S. Webb and Wm. Douglas. The affidavit is is also signed by Bartholomew Dandridge, Clerk of the County.

A pension of $8 per mo. was granted, to commence July 9, 1818; certificate was sent to Bartholomew Dandridge, Esq. Clerk of New Kent Co., this pension was suspended under Act May 1, 1820.

RICHARD DOBSON. (File No. S. 9386; certificate No. 23,322.) Dec. 12, 1833, when he was 70 years of age, Richard Dobson made affidavit before the judges of New Kent Co., Court, stating that he was born in New Kent County, Va., Merth 10, 1763 and had enlisted from that county Mch. 25, 1781 as a private in Capt. Hockaday's Co., for 2 mos. His 2nd enlistment was in Capt. Bacon's Co., for 2 mos., when he was placed on duty at the Forge in New Kent Co. His 3rd. enlistment, also for 2 mos., was in the Co. of Capt. Jarrett when he served in different places viz. the Siege of Yorktown; that he was one of the men detailed to guard the prisoners captured there and being taken to Winchester. He accompanied them as far as Hanovertown where Capt. Jarrett gave him a verbal discharge. Dobson stated he had always lived in New Kent Co., excepting for a period of 2 years when he lived in Hanover Co. He recollected Gen. Stevens, Col. Scot and Maj. Welsh being in command at Yorktown and Gen. Washington. He stated he was well known to Col. Wm. C. Clopton, Thomas Clopton, Frances Marshall, Beverly Crump and others of his county.

The Judges presiding at the New Kent Court that day were: Wm. H. Macon, Wm. Chamberlayne, John S. Lacy, Philomon Jones and Wm. Slator. John D. Christian was County Clerk at that time.(Dec. 12- 1833.)

Jonathan Silliman a clergyman of New Kent Co., Thomas Clopton of Henrico.Co., Wm. H. Macon (Judge) all testified to the honesty of Dobson and that they believed he had x served in the Revolution.

Pension of $20 per yr. was granted beginning Mch. 4, 1831. The certificate was sent to Hon. John Tyler of Chas. City Co., member of the Senate.

WILLIAM LADD. (File No. W 8079; certificate No. 25,282.) May 13, 1833 Wm. Ladd made affidavit before the Judges of New Kent Co., Court stating that he was then 73 years of age; had enlisted from that county 1, 4 1781 as a private in the Co. of Capt. Lyddal Bacon of New Kent Co., in the Regt. of Colo. Richmond Allen of sd, county; that he was marched to Providence Forge in sd. Co., where some of the regular troops were stationed under Command of Gen. Nelson and Maj. Ragsdale (during Arnold's invasion); thence marched under Capt. Joseph Holt to Williamsburg and then to Hampden, Va., where several barges or boats of the enemy were taken when they came to shore for the purpose of plundering. On Mch. 19, 1781 he returned home. In a few days he entered the service again under same Capt. Bacon until about May 1st., 1781, when he was again permitted to return home. June 30, 1781 he entered

REVOLUTIONARY PENSIONERS.

the service under Lieut. Jacob Vaiden, in Regt. of Colo. Richardson and was marched to Malvern Hills, Henrico Co., thence to Brook Bridge about 7 miles above Richmond, thence to Newcastle in Hanover Co., thence to the Brick House in New Kent Co. on the York River, and thence to the counties of King and Queen, Gloucester and Middlesex in which last named he was discharged-- Sept 9, 1781. At different times during the last enlistment he was under Cols. Taylor and Ennis. The 1st time he was called he was in Continental Line at Long Bridges in New Kent Co., under Gen. Nelson. The rest of his service was with the militia attached to the 3rd. Va. Regt. commanded by Cols. Taylor and Goodall. He stated that Samuel Moss and James Williams were the only ones in the county who could testify to his actual service. His service was about 7 mos. in all. He was born in New Kent Co., Feb. 8, 1760, and has always lived in that county.

Wm. H. Macon (Judge) testified to the good character of Wm. Ladd said he was sure he had served in the Rev. War although they were not together in the service. Macon said he had served also.

The presiding Judges were: Wm. H. Macon, R. Graves, B. Crump, Jones R. Christian and Thomas Macon. Jno D. Christian was County Clerk.

A pension of $20. a year was granted Sept. 11, 1833 the certificate being sent to E. Heath of Richmond.

Mary Ladd, widow of William Ladd made application for pension May 12, 1843. At that date she made affidavit before Nathaniel L. Savage, Justice of the Peace of New Kent Co., Va., stating that she was then 84 years old and that she was married to William Ladd in New Kent Co., by Parson Sample about the 17th of Dec. 1778 and that her husband, the sd. William Ladd had died May 9, 1843.

James Clopton of New Kent Co. made affidavit in Jan. 1845 before Wm. Slater, Justice of the Peace saying he was then 63 years of age and had known Wm. and Mary Ladd well when they lived in New Kent Co., and knew their children the eldest of whom was John Ladd who was exactly the same age as himself and they had gone to school together. He stated that Wm. and Mary Ladd were wise and respectable people of good standing in society and were surely married. The Judge, Wm. Slater testified to the character of James Clopton, Saying he was a Baptist Minister of that county and a "gentleman of h high respectability".

John D. Christian, Clerk of the county stated that the marriage record of Wm. & Mary Ladd which may have been in his office was no doubt destroyed with the other court papers that were burned in a fire of 1787. He said the will of Wm. Ladd was on record in his office and by it Mr. Ladd devised all of his estate to his wife Mary during natural life, and at her death it was to go to their children--- eight in number.

A widow's pension of $20. per anum was granted to Mary Ladd beginning March 3, 1843. The certificate of same (No. 6838) was sent to F. V. Sutton of Richmond, Va.

JOHN HILL. (File No. S. 38,026; certificate No. 3799.) May 15, 1818 when he was 67 years of age, John Hill appeared in court of New Kent County and testified that he enlisted in the Rev. War in Co. of King Wm., Va., Jan. 1778, as a private in the company of Capt. Henry Quarles of 2nd. Va. Regt. of Artillery on Continental establishment; was discharged Nov. 1780 at Hillsborough, North Carolina. He was in the battle of Camden.

The presiding Judges that day were: Ro: Warren, Jno. L. Poindexter, Beverly Crump and Seaton W. Crump. Bartholomew Dandridge was Clerk of the Co.

Sept. 14, 1820 John Hill again appeared in court and said he was 70 yrs. old on the 4th day of Feb. last.(evidently was born 2-4-1750) and a resident of New Kent Co., for---- years; that he enlisted for 3 years in the 2nd Va. State Regt. of Artillery under Col. Marshall and Capt. Henry Quarles. After serving sometime he exchanged places with a private named Lipscomb in the 2nd State Regt. of Musketry and went to the northward and served out Lipscomb's term in a Regt. commanded by Gregory Smith(Col?), H. Dabney as Lt. Col., and James Quarles as Capt., and received his discharge from Gen. Muhlenburg in 1778 near Middlebrook Mountain. He returned to Va.; found his 2nd. Va. Artillery Regt. and served out his own term of enlistment. He was in the battle of Camden and "ran like a good fellow"; got his discharge at Hillsborough, N. C., from Maj. Mazaret in 1780. He stated his trade was a planter and he was left-handed, but had lately injured his left hand, hence his great need for a pension. He stated he had a daughter, Betsy Hill, living with him, who was healthy and able to earn her living.

The Judges presiding at New Kent County Court on that day were: Jno. H. Christian, John L. Webb, Ro: Perkins & Wm. E. Clopton. Bartholomew Dandridge was County Clerk.

A pension of $96. a year was granted from Oct. 21, 1818.
John Hill died 8- 27- 1822.

JAMES WILLIAMS. (File No. 6506; Certificate No. 23760.) March 1834 James Williams appeared in Court of New Kent Co., Va., and testified that he was then 70 years of age, and had enlisted in the Rev. War from that county for a tour of 3 mos. service in the Co. of Capt. George Baker. His 2nd enlistment was under Capt. John Bacon when he was stationed at Providence Forge, New Kent Co., then marched to Yorktown where he changed Captains and was under Capt. Waldergrove Clopton who was from New Kent Co. They marched to "Newport nuse" at the mouth of the James River, then was returned to Yorktown whence his term expired and his Capt. having "quitted" he returned to his home, the tour having been about 6 mos. He recalled serving under Gen. Nelson, Col. Innis and Maj. Ragsdale. He said he was born in New Kent Co., in 1763 and had lived there all of his life excepting a short time that he lived in Richmond. (The signature of James Williams -- a very good one-- appears on this paper.)

The presiding Judges of Now Kent Court that day were: Wm. H. Macon, Ro: Graves, Beverly Crump, John Augustine Taylor and Thomas H. Terrel Jno. D. Christian was County Clerk.

Sept. 13, 1843 Pattey Williams, widow of James Williams, appeared before Jno. S. Lacy, Justice of the Peace in New Kent Co., and also a Justice of the County Court, and on oath stated that she was 78 years, 11 months and 10 days old, and a resident of New Kent Co. She said she and James Williams were married March 7, 1784 and that James Williams had died Sept. 29- 1840.

John K. Brodenham witnessed the above affidavit and Jno. S. Lacy, J.P. also signed it. Jno. D. Christian was County Clerk.

Sept 13, 1843 John Williams, son of James Williams, also appeared before Judge John S. Lacy and verified his mother's statements.

Dec. 20- 1843 Wilson Williams sent a certified declaration from Richmond.

Jan. 15, 1851 Richmond Williams a resident of King & Queen Co, Va., states he is 45 years of age, and writes a certified letter from that county stating he is his mother's "committee" and declares she is Mrs. Pattey Williams, the widow of James Williams, and that she is now 80 years old. (The signature of Richmond Williams-- an excellent one-- appears here.) These declarations are sworn to before Roderick Bland, J.P., and witnessed by Thomas J. Turner and Ro: P. Smith. Robert Pollard was County Clerk of .

King & Queen County. (In these declarations Pattey Williams is still called "of New Kent Co.") A small book is filed with these papers. Inside the cover is written "Family Register, drawn out of Bible March 24, 1792." On the next page: "James Williams, his book " and the family records follow:

"I was born Oct. 20- 1762
Pattey(my) wife bo(rn) October 3, 1764
we was married the 7th day of Mch 1784
1. John Williams born 1- 30- 1785
2. Dianor born 2- 23- 1787
3. Lucey born Oct 9, 1788
4. James Williams born Jan. 14, 1791
5. Josiah Williams born Oct. 10, 1794
6. Wilson born Sept. 30, 1796
7. Lorey born Sept. 17, 1798
8. Foster born Aug. 27, 1800
9. Patsy born Feb. 18- 1802
10. Richmond born Oct. 30, 1805
    Foster died May 8, 1816

SAMUEL MOSS. (File No. S. 8988.) May 13, 1833 Samuel Moss made affidavit before the Court of New Kent County,Va., declaring that he was then 69 years old: that he was born in New Kent Co. A record which he presented stated: "Samuel Moss, son of Samuel and Elizabeth was born May the 23rd 1764. " He further stated that he had always lived in that county. His 1st enlistment was 4 Jan. 1781 at Providence Forge as a private in Co. of Capt. Lyddal Bacon of New Kent Co., and the Regt. of Colo. Richmond Allen of sd. county. He stayed at the Forge about 10 days, then marched to Long Bridges in same county and later was sent under Capt. Joseph Holt to Williamsburg and thence to Hampton, Va. Later he served a short tour under Capt. Bacon. In June 1781 under Lieut. Jacob Vaiden and Col. Richardson he was marched to Melvern Hills in Henrico County. On this tour he also had service in King & Queen Co., Gloucester and at Brick House in New Kent Co., on the York River; was discharged in Middlesex Co., Va., about the 9th of Sept. 1781. He served under Cols. Taylor and Ennis. He enlisted again and was sent to Yorktown where he remained until the end of the siege. He was in the 2nd Regt. Va. Militia commanded by Cols. Taylor and Goodall. He had about 7 mos. service altogether.
James Clopton, a clergyman of New Kent Co., and William Ladd, James Williams and Judge Wm. H. Macon all testified to the character and veracity of Samuel Moss, and their firm belief that he had served in the Rev. as he said.
The presiding Judges of the Court were: Wm. H. Macon, Beverly Crump, Thos. Macon, John Augustine Taylor and Thos. Terrell. Jno. D. Christian was Co. Cl.
The death date of Samuel Moss is not known; but the agency was notified of his death Jan. 31, 1845.

EDWARD SLATER. (File No. S. 18, 205; certificate No. 23,709.) March 17, 1834 Edward Slater made affidavit before New Kent Co. Court that he was then 75 years of age and a resident of that county. He said he first enlisted in the Rev. as a militiaman under Capt. Baker in the Regt. of Colo. Richmond Allen, and was sent to Williamsburg where he remained about 6 weeks. Later he was sent to Half-Way House in Eliz. City Co., Va., under Capt. George Ball of New Kent Co., and in about 10 days was marched to Staunton, Va., under Capt. Baker where he served about 8 mos. and was discharged. He was born in New Kent Co., in 1759.
James Clopton, a clergyman, John Breeding, James Williams and Judge Wm.H.Macon all of New Kent Co., testified to the character and veracity

REVOLUTIONARY PENSIONS.

of Slater and stated they firmly believed he had served in the War.
        The presiding Judges were: W. H. Macon, R. Graves, B. Crump,
J. A. Taylor and T.H.Terrell. Jno. D. Christian was Co. Clerk.

RICHARD WRIGHT. (File No. S. 39,922; certificate No. 3796.) May 15, 1818 when he was 66 years of age, Richard Wright made affidavit in New Kent County Court declaring that he was a resident of that county, and had enlisted in the service of the U.S. during the Rev. War, in Hanover Co. Va. Feb. 1777 as a private in the Co. of Capt. Benj. C. Spiller of the 2nd. Va. Regt. of Continental establishment; serving in sd. corps until Feb. 1780 when he was discharged at Falmouth, Va. He was in the Battles of Monmouth & Stoney Point,
        The Judges presiding on that day were: Richard Graves, Jno. L. Poindexter, Seaton W. Crump and Wm. Douglas. Bartholomew Dandridge was County Cl.
        A pension of $96 per year was granted Oct 21, 1818; certificate was sent to Hon. John Tyler of Eliz. City Court House, a member of the Senate.
        On Oct. 12, 1820 Richard Wright again made affidavit in New Kent Court saying he was then 71 years of age; had enlisted for 3 yrs. service in Feb. 1777 in Co. of Capt. Benj.Spiller of Colo. Chas Dabney's Va. Regt. of Continental establishment. He served until 1780 at which time he was under command of Capt. Tok and Colo. Dabney. His property consists of; 3 cows, 2 calves, 7 hogs, 3 pigs, 7 old chairs, 3 old bee gums, 7 old fish barrells, 1 pr. cards, 2 water vessels, 1 flat iron, 4 bottles, 2 boxes, 2 pots, 4 hoes, 2 fat pots, 2 ploughs, 1 foot adz chissel and drawing knife, 2 saws, 1 peck measure, 1 hoe, 1 tumbul cart, 13 turkeys. He is a planter but from infirmity not able to pursue this work; was previously a shoemaker but poor sight makes it impossible to do this anymore. He says he has 6 in the family; 5 are females his wife being one of them and "unable to help herself". The others, his daughters and work for themselves excepting one who waits on her infirm old mother.
        The Judges presiding at court that day were: John L. Poindexter, William Ratcliffe, R. Graves. Geo. Goddin & Wm. E. Clopton. Bartholomew Dandridge was County Clerk.
        Richard Wright died Jan. 27, 1822.

ROBERT POLLARD. (File No. W. 811.) Nov. 14, 1833, when 73 years of age, Robert Pollard appeared in New Kent Court and stated he had entered the service of the U.S. in the summer of 1779 as a drafted militiaman from Hanover Co. under Capt. John Stanley and was sent to Williamsburg; served 3 mos. From May to Oct. 1780 he marched from Hanover Co on a southern tour under command of Capt. John Price and Colo. Holt Richeson. He was in the Battle of Camden, S.C. After that battle he was transferred to the Co. of Capt. Parke Goodall, and was discharged at Guilford Ct. house in N.C.; had been in the service on this tour for 6 mos. In May 1781 marched again from Hanover Co., under Capt. Thomas Richardson, to Richmond; from there he patrolled up and down the James River; was in the skirmish at Osborn where the British destroyed several American vessells; after that was marched to Chas. City Court House; was in the service this time 3 mos. In the Spring of 1782 marched again from Hanover Co under Capt. Ambrose Lipscombe to guard and carry British prisoners from Gould Hill near Hanovertown to Winchester in Frederick Co., Va. This tour was 2 months. He was born in New Kent Co., Va., Jan. 12, 1760. When called to the service he was a resident of Newcastle, Hanover Co. Soon after the war he removed to New Kent Co., where he has resided ever since. He said Gen. Wm. Chamberlayne and his neighbors generally would testify as to his character, and those who remember the Rev. War can testify of his service.
        James Clopton, the Baptist minister of New Kent, and Samuel Keiningham also of New Kent testified to

REVOLUTIONARY PENSIONERS.

Pollard's honesty, etc. The presiding Judges were: Wm. H. Macon, Thos Macon, John F. Christian; Philemon C. Jones. Jno. D. Christian was Clerk of the County. The pension was granted for $46.66 a yr. on Dec. 11, 1833.

    Sackville Thacker of Louisa Co., made oath before Milton M. Brown, J.P. of Hanover Co., that he had served in the war and Pollard was with him.
    Joseph Spicer of Louisa Co., made oath before M.M. Brown, J.P. saying he was in Capt. Price's Co., also and marched on the southern tour; therefore endorsing Pollard's claim.
    Edward Cason of Spotsylvania Co. made oath before M. M. Brown, J. P. saying he also was in Capt. Price's Co.
    Wm. Bampass of Hanover Co., made oath before Parke Street, J.P. of said county saying he was on the tour to Richmond and down the James.
    Philip B. Winston was County Clerk of Hanover Co.(Nov. 1833.)
    James Wilkins of New Kent Co., 66 Yrs. old(Nov. 1833) testified that his father returning from Williamsburg one time during the war, brought with him Mr. Pollard who had his knapsack and had all the appearances of a soldier, and said he was returning to his home in Hanover Co after a tour of duty in the army. This affidavit was made before Judge Philemon Jones.
    Parke Street of Hanover Co. mails the declaration of Robert Pollard of New Kent to the Sec'y of War and puts in a note saying, he is doing this because there is no P.O. near Mr. Pollard's home, while one is at his door. He says he thinks the Sec'y ought to know that Mr. Pollard has 13 children and is badly in need of pension. He requests that mail be sent in his care: "Parke Street, Old Church, Hanover Co., Va."
    From Henrico Co., Va., Feb. 3rd 1853,-- Susanna Pollard, widow of Robert applies for a pension. Apr. 19, 1853 Jno. D. Christian, Co. Clerk writes from New Kent that he finds in his office a bond executed on Feb. 9th 1804 by Robert Pollard with James Finch as security payable to John Page, esq. Gov. of Va. saying a marriage license has been issued that day to Robert Pollard and Susanna Howle.
    Before Judge Binford of Henrico Co.(Apr. 21, 1853) Susanna Pollard, Resident of Henrico Co. and 67 years old says she married Robert Pollard Fe. 10, 1804, and he died July 17, 1835.

INDEX   A.

ACRE: Sarah 1; ACREE(or ACRU): Eliza. 18, John 18,Wm.18; ADAMS; Ann S.
20, Dematins 20, Epaphroditus 1, Fleming 46, John 1, 20, Lucy 43, Mary 20,
Mitchell 14, Peter 1, Richard 20, Robert E. 20, Watkins 14, William 20;
ALLEN: Edmund H. 17, Edward W. 17,Eliza D. 17, James 1, James Junr. 1,
James H. 44, John G. 1, John W. 17, Lucy D. 17, Paulina 1, 17,Richard 1,
Colo.Richmond 57,59,62, Sarah A.17, Thos. W. 17, Wm 1; AMEY 1; ANDERSON: Ann
52, Eliza A.14, Ellen 14,Emuella 15,James 1,14,John 1,John H. 15, John P.52,
Matilda A.15, Samuel C 14, Sarah 14,Wm. 15, Willianna 15; APPERSON: Ann E.39
Anne R. 30, Benj.F 53, Major D. 55, Edmund 1, Edward W.47,Eliz.M.30,Jno.C.
47, Littleberry 1,Maria B.30,Martha A.M.30, Martha L.30 Mary L.30, Polly 1,
Richard 1,Richard C.30, Ro.C.47, Ro.S.30, Sam'l H.47, Susan M.47, William 1,
Wm.A.47; ARMISTEAD: Guy 1,Robert B. 1, Susan A. 47, Wm 1,Willianna 47,
ASHWELL: Mary 1; ATKINSON: Dan'l O. 46, Eliz.F.46,Eliza R.33,Frances,A.33,
40,Geo.A 46, Georgianna 33, Henry W. 33, James 1,James M.31,James S.33,
John 39, Jno.T.33, Joseph 39,Lucy A. 40, Martha 39, Mary 1,Mary E.33,Mary W.
33, Rebecca 33, Richd. 40, Ro. W.H.33,Sally G.38, Susan A.46, Thos.W.49,
Turner 27, William 39,Wm.A. 40, Wm E. 46, Wm.V.49; AUSTIN: Coley 25,
Christopher 40,Delaware 40,Geo.W.40, Henrietta 39, James 39,Jas.T.42,
John 1,Julius H.1,Launcelot 40,Leroy L.43,Lucy 39,42,Martha E.43,Mary 39,
Mary A.E.43, Mary F.39,Rebecca 40,Richard 1,Susan 33,Thos.W.40,Wm 40,
Zachariah 1, Zac. 42; AYRES: John C. 1.

BACON: Capt.59,Elizabeth 2, Ferdinand 18,Harriet 18, Capt.John 57,61,
Capt. Lyddal 59,62,Wm E. 18; BAILEY: Anne E. 49, Ansalem 58, Anselm,Sr.2,
Anselm.Jr. 2, Anselm 51, Ballard D. 51,Eliz.R.27,Frances 27,Frances D. 11,
Geo.P.49, James 2,Jane 2, Letitia 49, Martha 51,58, Martha F. 51,Mary F.
49,Mary W. 51, Nancy 51, Rebecca 58, Sally P.49, Samuel 58, Tempey 53,Wm.1,
Capt. William 2,Wm Jr.2; BAKER: Capt.62, Elizabeth 57, Frances 57,Capt.Geo.
57,61,John 2, Richard 1,2,57, son Richard 57, Sarah A.21;BALL: Ann M.45,
Betty W.45,Elijah 45,Eliza 34, Capt.Geo.62,George 2,Indianna 34, Jno.34,
Lewellen 45, Martha A. 45, Mary J.45, Parkes 2,Perrien 34, Rebecca 45,
Walter 34, Wm.H.45; BAMPASS: Wm. 64; BANKS: Matilda 45,Nat.45,Ro.45,Virginia
45; BARHAM: Frances 25, Thomas 54; BARKER: Bailey 15, Dolly 18,Edney B.18,
John 2, 21,Henry 15,Martha 15,18, Octavia 15,Richard 55, Salley 2,William
21; BANES: John Sr. 4, William 4; BARKWELL: Thomas 2; BASSETT: Burwell,2;
BATKINS (or BOTKINS or BATHINS): Ann E. 51,Benj.M. 15, Betsey 27, Emiley 15,
Gilson,Agt. 48,Geo.W. 15, Harriet E. 15, Joseph 27, Julia A.13,Lucy B.15,
Martha J. 48, Martha W.48, Mary Ann 15, Ro. 51,48,Ro.B.48, Sally 2,Susan V.51
BATTS: Morris 8; BENFORD;George 2, Robert 2, BENN: Amanda 47, Ann 47, Emeline
47, George 47, Junius 47,Thos 47; BENNETT: Charles W. 19, Margaret K.19
Wesley P. 19; BENTLEY: Capt.57; BERLIMEYER: John O. 1; BETTY: 1; BERNARD:
Matilda 33; BINFORD: Judge 64; BINGLEY: Eliz. 26, Eliza 26, James 26,John
26, Virginia 26, Wm.J. 26; BINNS:Adelaide B. 51, Ambrose W. 42, Amelia W.42
Amelia A. 51,Amelia A.C.42,Charles 1,51,Chs.D.42,Chas.H.Jr.51,Chs.H.51,
Daniel 2, David 2; Frances C.42,Geo.56, Isaac 56,James E. 52, Jeremiah 2,
Jeremiah Jr.2,John 2,23,Kitty 56,Marston,2,Martha 2,Martha E.51,Martha P.23,
Mary C.51, Mary Jane 56,O.P.42, O.P.Jr.42,Richard 2,Sam 54,56,Susan 56,
Washington 56,Wm E.23,51;BIRCH: Mary 1, Milley 1,Reuben 2; BIRD: Sam 2;
BLAND: Roderick J.P.61 BLAYTON: James S.44, Jno.H.44,Maria 44,Maria W.44,
Mary T.44,Wm A.26;BOND: Eliz.53, Emily 53, Martha 53,Mary C.53, Wm.53;BONE:
Hezekiah 2,BOSMAN: Benskin 2,James 2; BOSWELL: Ann E. 42, Edward 38,Hester A.
37,John 2, 38 John,L.42, Jno.T.43,John W.39 Jas.W.43,Joseph 38, Lucinda 39,
Lucy 38,Lucy J.38,Martha A.38,Mary E.42, Mary F.38,Nancy 40,Richard 38, Sarah
39,Susanna 42,Tabithy,38, William 1,Wm.G.43, Wm.J.38,Wm.S.42; BOWIS or
(BORVIS): Allen W.33,Barbara Anna 16, Betty 16, Cath A, 46, Edward A. 16,
Geo.B.P. 16, Georgella 16, Jesse Scott, 2,Jno.R.46,Julia A. 16, Mary E.46,
Mary I. 16, Ro.L.46, Sally P. 16, Stanhope,M.46,Wm 2, Wm A.46; BOWERS:

B.

John 2; BOWLES: Ira L.39, BOYD: Alwilda C. 14, Earl 14,George G.14,John P 14 Martha I. 14, Robert 1,Sally B. 14,William 1,William R. 14;BRADENHAM: Eliz.A. 30, Eliza 30,Eliza A.30,James E. 30,John K.61,Jno R.30,Mary R.30, Robert.2. BRADLEY: Anne 2, Anne M. 51, Edward 2,45,Eliz.45, George 45, Georgiana 45, James M. 54, Lucy L. 51, Lutilda 45,Maria L.45,Martha 45,Mary 45,Mary E.54 Mary L.51,Mitchell W.50,Nancy 45;Pleasant 2,Ro.45,Sarah 24,Susan 45,Wm.45; BRAXTON: Abram 2; BREEDING: Harriet 31,John 2,57,62,Julius 2,Wm.29; BREWELL: Wm.2; BROOKES: Sam 2. BROUGHTON: Polley 13,; BROWNE (and BROWN): Ann 38, Jane 40, John 2,57, Mary E.40,Milton M.(J.P.) 64, Octavia 40,Ro.T.40, Susan F.40; BURMLEY: George D. 13; BURNETT: Frances E. 19, Garland A.27,James 25,27, John 27, Jno. H. 19, Jos. 43, Julia A. 25, Kitty 25, Lavinia 27, Lucy A. 19,41, Mary 20,Mathew H. 19, Mathew W. 19, Peyton 25, Reuben 25, Sarah 25, 41, Wm.A.41,William D. 19,Wm.W. 28, Wilson 18;BURTON: Lucy T. 16;BURWELL: Billy 45.

CALL:Eliz. 39, Lewis 39, Lucy A. 39, Susan 39, Wm. 39; CAMBO: Nelson 3 CAPADA: Patsey 24; CARLO: John Jr. 2; CARTER: Eliz.B.23,Lutilda L. 51, Margaret A. 51, Maria L.51, John 3,John G.51,John G.Jr.51,Richd.D. 51, Ro.F. 23; CASEY: Martha 31; CASON: Edward 64; CHADICK: Cath.E. 20, Maria L.20,Martha A.20,James 20,John I.20,Sarah A.20,2A, Sarah E.21,Thos.D.21,Wm.T.21; CHAMBERLAYNE: Edw.P. 13, Gen. Wm. 63,Wm.3,59, CHANDLER: D.P.39,Edwd.53, Emma 54,Georgianna W.33, Harman 53, Hester 54, James 4,41,54,Jno.F.41,Jos.41,Martha 25,Mary 54, Mary A.41,Mary A.E.33,Mary A.W.33, Miles M.33, Oliver M.54, Richard 3, Robert B.39, Susan 54, Theo.L.39, Thomas B.3. Vandalia 41, Wm.3,Wm.H. 54; CHAPMAN: Benj. 25; CHAPPELL (and CHAPPEL): Benjamin 3, 59, Carrell Fleming 58, Eliz. 20, Henry 20, Patsey 20,Winchester,3; CHOPELAND: Michael 3; CHRISTIAN: Agness 3,Amelia C.48, Ann 48, Ann E. 52, Archer 3, Armistead 55, Augustine 55, Bat. D. 12, 55, Betty I. 52, Caroline N. 52, Collier 3, Chris.S. 52, Christiana 52, Edmd. C.52, Edmd. F.52, Elizabeth 52, Eliz.C.48, Eugenia 52, Gideon 3, Henry B.52,James 55, James C. 51, James S. 55, John D. 55, 59,60,61, 62, Jno.F. 48, John H. 3,51,57,58,59, Jones R. 3,52,60, Lucy 51,Maria L.48, Martha M.51,Mary M.52,Octavia St.C. 55, Robert 3,52,58, Sarah A.52, Semll.P.48 William 55, Wm C.52,Wm.E.52; CLAIBORNE: Thomas 3,Wm.B.38, CLARKE: Alice J.28 And. W.33,Major And. 28, Charles,4,David W.28, David 3, Eliz.C.33, Eliz.F.40, Fred W.28, Freeman,G. 15,George W. 28, Harriet S 28,Jas W.33, Jesse 3,John 3, 28,33, Lotsey F.28, Martha 53, Martha R.28, Mary A.33,Mary E. 33, Mary W.28, Polly 55, P.-W. 42, Rebecca 33, Richard A. 42, R.Dand.28, Ro.S. 33,Susan E. 28, Wm. 3, Wm.A.28, Wm R.47; CLAYTON: Eliza. T.47, Fanny C.47, Jasper A.47, Jasper A.Jr.48, Wm.B.48, Wyatt,H.48; CLOPTON: Edwin,3,Edwin I. 15, Edwin I.Jr. 15, H.D. 15, James 2.60, 63, John 2, John Sr. 3,Rev. John B.58, Maria 15,Mary 21, Mary E.C. 15, Mary I.21, Mary S.51, Thomas 59, Wm.3, Col.Wm.C.59, Wm.E. 61, 63,Wm.R.3,Waldergrave,3,Capt. Waldergrove 61; COCKERHAM: Edward 3; COOKE: Alice A.49, Ann E,39, Margaret C.39, Mary A.39, Mary E.39,Octavia R. 49, Richd.D.49, Richard P.39, Sarah E. 39,Wm.4, Wm.C.49, COOPER: Jesse 3; COSBY: Charles 3, John 2; COUCH:Emily 38, Hester,A.38, Isaac 38,James W.38, John W. 38,Mary 38, Ro.K.38,Sarah. A. 38; COURTNEY: Benj.18,Martha A.18, Mary 18, Naomi 18,Robert 18,Selina 18, Wm.H.18,Wm.H.Jr.18; CRABBIN: Ann 48, Eliz.47, Emiley 47, Dyonisia 47, James 48, Jesse 47, John 46, 48, Judith 49, Lucy 48, Sally 47, Susan 48, Thos.48,Wm B.49; CRAWLEY: Wm.3; CRENSHAW: Judge Ed.B.58; CRITTENDEN: Sally 3, CROW: Anthony 3, James,3, Jesse 3; CROWDIR. John D.46, Maria L. ,46, Martha F.46, Miles C.46, Sarah C.46,Sarah M. 46; CRUMP: Abner 3, Capt.Abner 58, Alice A.28,Anderson 3,24, Anne 3, Ann E.42, Ann L. 54, Ann W.43,Annette 28,Augustine 47, Bartle,27, Benedict3, Beverley 3, 54,57,59, 60,61,62, Burton 27, Camilla S.24,Cath.41,Chr.M.24,Charles C.47, C.I.24,Christopher 2, Columbus 24,Cornelius 24,David S.M.28, David W.28, Edgar, M. 28,Edmund 2, E.G.47, Eliz P.54, Elizabeth 38, Eliz.E.28, Eliz.S.34, Emiley A.47, Fielding H.15, Fleming T.17, Frances B.27,George 27,38, Geo.P.24,47; George T.42 Hammond F.33,Henry C.24, James 3 James D.18, John 3,24,38,John C.3,John G.42, Jno.Lewis P.24,John P.3,Jno.S.28,Jos.T.P.38,Jno.W.34, Jesse 2,Jo.I.38, Josephine 24,Josiah 2,Lawrence S.28,Lemuel 33,Leonard C.47, Lucy P.42, Margaret B.27, Margaret H.54,Maria S.42,Martha 27,38, Martha E. 17,

Mary 28, 42, Mary A. 28, Mary B.24, Mary C.24, 47, Mary F.42, Mary I.24, Mary J. 24, Matilda H.24, Nathaniel 3, Pat.H.34, Richard.3,24,43, Ro.47, Ro.D.24, Sallie B.47, Sarah 38, 33, Sarah E.17, Seaton,W. 57, 60, Spencer C.24, Susan E.B.24 Sylvanus G.42, Thomas.2, Virginia B.42, Will 3, William 3,38, Wm.A.24, Wm.B.42, Zac. T. 24; CRUTCHFIELD: John 3; CUMBER: Ann 44, Benj. 44, Henry 44, Isanna 44, Martha 44, Melville 44, Nelson 44, Savannah W.37, Seaton,M.44, Sophia T.36, Thos.E.37, Wm.N.36; CURLE: Benet 3, David 3, John 4, Jno.S.33, Richardson, 3, Sarah A.37; CURTIS: B.A. 51, CUSTIS: Geo.W.P. 3.

DABNEY: Colo. Chas.63, Lt.Col.H.61; DANDRIDGE: Bartholomew 3,4,23, 57,59,60,61, Eliz. W. 23, John B.54, Wm A.23, Willinette R.23; DANGEY: Isabella 4; DANIEL: Fanny 21, Parke 4; DAVIS: Anthony 1,4, Frances E. 27, Hugh L.27 John 4, Mary 27, Tho.W.27, Wm.P.49; DAY: Wm. W. 4; DEBRISS: Wm.44; DENNETT: Catharine 4, Chs. 53, James 4, 53, Richard 4, Ro.48, Sarah 53, Wm.L. 53. DIGGS Isaac 4, John W. 26, Thos.A.26; DILLARD: Edward 4, James M. 53; DIXON: Edward 4, Eliz. 49, Eliza A.49, James 49, Jane S.49, Jno.R. 49; Julius C.41, Mary A. 49, Mary C.41, Thos.S.49, Wm J.49, William R. 42. DOBSON: John 18, Mary 18, Richard,4, 59, DOUGLAS: Eliz.Joan 52, Henry T.52, John B.52, Lucy A.52, Mary 52, William 4, 57, 58,59, Wm.R.C. 52, Wm Walter 52, DOW: Robert 4; DOZIER: William 13; DRAKE: Ro. 44, Wm.44. DRINKARD: William 4, DUDLEY: Eliza 31; DUNGAY (or Dungee) : Reuben 4, Pamelia I.27; DUNN: Mildred 53, Mildred A.53; DUNSFORD: Emily 31, Jno. 31, Jno.E. 31, Mary 31, Mary C. 31, Matilda 31, Rebecca 31.

EAMES: Emeline 40, Frances 35, James L.35, Joel 4, Joel W. 35, John Jr. 4, Judith 35, Letter A.35, Octavia 40, Pleasant W.35, Wm.R.40; EARNEST: Roseanna D. 18; EASTER: Sally 4; EATON: J.H. 58; EGGLESTON: Richard S. 30; EGGMAN: Christopher 4; Ellett; Beverley 16, Cornelius 16, Lucy Ann M. 16, Sarah 16, William T. 16; ELLYSON: Agness 4, Alfred B.22, Alice 22, Betty F. 14, ? Collier H.22. Daniel 22, David 4, Ellen 22, Elizabeth 14, Emeline 22, Gideon 4, Havilah T. 14, Havilah 14, Helen 22, Henrietta 22, James 22, Jesse 4, Jonathan 4, Julia 22, Julia A.22, Lemuel G. 14, Louisa 22, Margaret 4, Marjery 22, Martha 22, 54, Mary D.22, Nancy A. 14, Rebecca 22, Richard 22, Sam 22, William P. 14; ENNIS (or Innis) Col. 60, 61, 62, ENOS: James 30; EPPES: Ann 23, Edward 23, Jane E. 23, John T. 23, Sally A. 23; EVANS: James 4, 36, Mary A.W. 36 36, Nancy 36, Sarah 26,

FARRIS (or FARIS) Jacob 4, John 4, Sylvanus 4, Wm.4; FARINHOLT: Avery G.26, Eliz. 26, Geo.L.28, Harriet 28, John 28, Luther 28, Louisa 28, Mary E. 26, Ro.A.28; FARTHING: Garico,H.29, Inez. R.29, Mahala F.29, Maria L. 29, Presiosa E.29, Susan W.29, Wm H.29, FIDDLER: Mary A.E.33, Wm. A.33; FIELDS: John 4; FILRATES: Benj. 36, Cornelius 32, Eleanora 32, Harriet L. 32, Lucy 32 Mary 36, Tho. 36, Wm.36, Wm.Jr.36; FINCH: James 4, 64, Samuel 4, Wm 4; FINLEY Wm.26; FIRBUSH: Thomas 5, FIRTH: John 5, Samuel 5; FISHER Ann M.24, Geo.W. 24, FLEMING: Capt.John 59, FORD: Lucy A.46, Mary 46, Wm. 46; FOSTER: Jesse 4, Joseph 4, Josiah 30, Peter C. 16, Capt.Peter 58, Rachael G.30, Sarah E.30, W.M.L.30; FOX: James 4, Nathaniel 4; FRANCES: John 4; FRANCISCO: Peter 58, FRANKS: Amanda T.41, Eliz. 41, John 4, Jno.D. 41, Jno O. 41, Rebecca 41, Virginia 41, FRAYSER: Beverley 4, Collier C.47, Elvira 4, Elvira C.21, Phila.P.21, Rebecca 24, Richd. E. 54; FREEMAN: Sally 5, FRENCH: Frances E. 13, Lucretia 13, Martha A.C. 13, Polly D. 13, Portia 13, Thomas 13, Thomas I. 13, FURGERSON, Frances 4, FURLONG: Alexander 4; FUSSILL(or FUSSELL): Aaron 19, Frances W.22. Jno. T. 22, Mary 22. Mary T. 22.

GALLING: Samuel 5, Samuel Jr. 5; GARLICK: Braxton, 14, Henrietta 14, James H. 14, Mary C. 14, Medora B. 14; GARNETT: Cath. B.28, Cath. C. 28, James 5, Ro. A.28, Wm.M.28; GARRETT: Jno. I. 36; GATHRIGHT: Lucy 15, Martha 50,

Page C

D.

Robert 5; GARY: Benj.D.24, Edwin J.48, James 5, Jno.F. 48, Marietta 24, Mary E. 48, Mathew 24, Rebecca 48, Ro.F.48, Sarah A.24, Servatus 48, Susanna F. 48, Theo.I. 48, Willenette 24; GERRY: James F. 48; GEDDIN: Avery 5; GEDDY: William 5; GENNINGS: Sally 5; GEORGE: Bird, 5, GIBSON: Col. George 58, Jeduthon 5; GILLIAM: Elizabeth 40, Elizabeth E. 40, Emeline C. 40, Edaphroditus 5, Eppa D. 41, Fanny 41, Frances 5, Frances A. 40, James C. 40, Jno.S. 40, Margaret J.41, Maria S. 40, Martha I.W. 40, Richd. S. 41, Ro. A. 40, Rufus T.40, Sarah F. 41, Thos Q. 40, Wesley 41, Wm.O. 40; GLASS: David 5, GLAZEBROOK: Betsy 44, Cynthia 44, Jas. 44, James Jr. 5, Joseph 29, Mary 44, Richard 44; GOODALL: Col. 60, 62, Capt.Parke, 60; GLENN: Eliz. 38, John 5, 38, Mary 49; GODDIN: Geo. 63, Geo.P.32, James,H. 32, James N.32. Mary A. 32, Sylvanus 32; GODFREY: 5, GOODE: Alena F. 18, Cath. C. 19, Jos H. 19, Lucy F. 18, Wm. Jr. 18, Wm. B. 18; GOODMAN: Agnes,A. 21, Angelica 33, Benj. 21, Benj. E. 21,Charles H.21,Elizabeth 5, Jas. E. 21,Jno.H.33, Leroy D. 21, Louisa V. 21,Maria A. 21, Nancy,42, Sarah E. 33, Thomas 47, Virginia A. 33, Wm.M. 21,33, Govan(or GORAN): James 13, Lucy A. 13; GOWER: Stanley P.5. GRANT: Clarissa 16, James C. 16, Cath. 16, GRAVES: Edmund 5, James S. 45, R. 60 60, Richard 5, 63, Robert 57, 58, 61, GREEN: Edward 5, Eliz 46, Maria D. 46, Wm 5, Wm A 46; GREGORY: William 5; GRIGGS: Mary 41, Richard 41.

HALL: Richard 5, HALSEY: Isaac 6, HALYBURTON: Wm. 6, HAMLET: Burwell 5; HARDEN: Mathew J.54; HARMAN: Anne E.43, Benj.43. Elizabeth 5, Ishamar 5, James 26, John 5, John Jr. 6, John P1 26, Keziah 5, Larkin 44, Leroy 44, Martha 44, Martha A.43, Martha J.43, Mary 26, Micajah 35, Sally H. 43, Susan 44, Turner 44, Wm.G. 43, Wm.44, Hazwell: Jas.C. 43, Mary F. 43, Washington 43; HEATH: E. 60; HERBART: Anthony 5, HEWLETT: C.A. 17, Maria L. 17, Mary F. 17, Matilda B. 17; HIGGINS: Ann.E. 16, Catharine 22, Eliza 20, Elizabeth 20, 21,Eliz H. 16, Foster 6, Jornn 20,John 20, 21, Jos. F.21,
Joshua 22, Josiah 5, Josiah Sr. & Jr. 16, Maria L.20, Martha A. 15, Mary 22, Mathew 58, Mathew A.21,Miles 22, Nancy 22, Pat.H.20, Poindexter 20, Rosalin 22, Saml.D. 21,William 22; HILL: Almira 14,Augustine 14, Bat. 18, Elizabeth 29, George 24, Jas.M. 29, John 5, 61, John G. 29, John T. 17, Josephine T. 17, Julia A.29, Julian A.29, Juliet I. 14,Harriet C.14, Martha A. 14,Martha I. 14, Parkes, 6, Richard A. 17, Ro. A 14, Tabitha 17, Wm.24, William 55; HANKINS (or HABKINS): Cleopatra L.25, Geo.22, Lucy M. 25; HILLIARD: Benskin 5, Benskin H. 5, Benskin M. 35, Cynthia 35, Eliz 33. Isaac M.33, John 5, Mary 6, Richard 5, Thomas 6, Wm.E. 35, HIX. Ahaz.33, Andrew 29, Alice 31, Benj.44, Betsy 17, Cynthia 36, Edward 5, Eliz. 27, 36, George 5, John 6, 29, 44, Jno. R. 29, Martha 44, Mary 27, Mary F.29, Nancy 36,Nathaniel 6, Rebecca 25, 36, Sheppard 27, Susan 29, William 5, 30, 33, Wm. M. 29; HOCKADAY: Capt. 59, Edmund 6, Eliza 31, Eliza A. 31,Eliz.54, 17, Eliz. R. 32, Eliz. W. 30, Jno.A. 32, Jno.R. 31, Judith,W. 31, Juliet 54, Martha 17, Mary 31, Mary B.32, Philmer, 17, Richard 17, Richard W. 31, Sally 6, Sarah 32, Sarah C. 31, Wm 5, Wm O.32, HOGAN: Walter P.49, Hollins: Delphis 5, HOLSWORTH: Elizabeth 5; HOLT: Capt.Joseph 59, 62, William 6, HOOMES: Amos, 6, HOPKINS: And. J. 43, Ann E. 43, Edward R. 43, James B.17, James M.43, Mary F. 43, Priscilla 5, Thos. 43; HOUCHING: Andrew 46, Benj.F. 47, Eliz. 47, James 16, Jno 46, 47, Sarah A. 47, Silas 47; HOWARD: Eliz I. 29, James M. 29, Wm.H.29, HOWLE: Ann V. 23, Charles 5, Daniel 5, Delia A.27 Edmund W. 23, Geo.W. 46, Gideon 6, Henry I.46, Isaac 6, 46,55, James 56, Janetta 27, John 5, John G.48, John W.27, Lewis 5, Martha A. 50, Mary 5, 46, Mary H. 55, Ro. 55, Susan 27, Susanna 64, Susan F.23,Thomas 6; HUBBARD: Benj.C. 27, Bowler,27,Jno.S.27, Jos,C. 27,Lucy A.27, Pamelia F.27,Wm N.27, HUGHES: Elizabeth 5, James 18, Martha 34, Mary 40, Nancy 35, Reuben 21; HUXSTEP: John 13, HYLTON: John 6,

E.

INGRAM: Wm. G. 6, ISON: Maria 29, Ro. 29, Wm. 29.

JACKSON: Aaron 6; JAIL 54; JAMES: Ann 6; JARRETT: Capt. 59; JEFFERY 6; JERDONE: Ro. P. 18; JOHNSON: Ann B. 13, Cath. 49, David 6, Joseph 18,18, Lucy Ann 13, Maria E. 13, Polly 18, William 6; JENNINGS: Adias 50, Emiley 32, Isaac S. 50, Isaac 50, James K.P. 32, John W. 32, Laura F.32, Major R. 32, Martha 50, Martha A. 32, Mary B.26, Mary J. 50, Mary T. 33, Os.T. 50, Ro. S.26 32, Sarah I.26, Spencer 32, Susan 26, Wm 50, Wm P.49, JONES: A.G.49, Albina R. 25, Amanda B.37, Ann 25, Burwell,B. 36, Charles 6, Chs. R. 37, Chesley 6,35, Chesley M.25, Chesley R. 25, Cillar, 6, Cornelia 32, Daniel 6, Daniel M. 25, Delia 25, 32, D.N.35, Drusilla B.37, Edmond T. 18, Elizabeth 6, Eliza 36, 35, Ellen T. 25, Frances R. 37, H.B.37, James 35, Leuversa 35, Lewis 25, Lucy A. 37, Lucy B.37, Lucy C.37, Maria 36, Martha A. 25, 35, Martha L.25, Martha V.R. 25, Martha W.37, Nancy 6, 35, Nelson 6, Octavia 25, Pamelia 25, Philemon 59, Judge Philemon 64, Philip C.25, Randolph 35, Rebecca 35, Robert 6, Robert E. 6, Rowland 37, Rowland A. 37, Vernon 36, Willentina 36, William 6, 25,35,William Jr. 6, Wm.A. 37, Wm N. 25, Wm.T. 25,

KENINGHAM: Benj. 6, Samuel 6, 63, KELLEY: James H.20, KENT: Betsy 46, Nancy 46, Thomas 6, Williiam 6, KILBY: John T. 6; KIRKMYER: Wm. 35; KNEWSTEP: Amanda B.31, Ann 26, Archer 26, Eliz. 35, Fred 35, Fred C. 35, George 35, Harriet 31, Leonida 31 Lucy M. 31,Miles 31, William S. 31, KNIGHT: Wm; KUNNINGHAM: Betsy 23.

LACY: Ann. E. 49, Arch E. 49, Archibald 7, Bacon 7, Barthol. 50, Benj. W. 54, Betty W. 54, Ed.B.28, Eliza E. 50, Ellen G. 54, Geo.R. 50, Harriet 2l 28, Jno B 36,, John C. 50, John S. 36, 61, Lane 54, Mary 6, Mary A. 50, Nora B.49 49, Philemon 6, Rich. B.50, Richard T. 54, Richmond T. 54, Sally E. 54, Sally H. 36, S. O.49,Stephen 6, Susan A.E. 40, Theo.A. 49, Theo H 54, Theo S.49, Wm.7, LADD: David 7,James 6, 46, John 7, Mary 60, Wm 7, 59, 60, 62, LAYFAYETTE: James 6; LAMBETH: George 44, John 44, Rosalie 44, Sarah 44, Thomas 44, LANGLEY: Henry B.7, John W. 7, Wm 7, LAWSON: Wm.7, LESTER: Benj.F.37, Betsy 34, John B.37, Lucy R.37, LEWIS: Ann E.48, BURDETTA 7, Catey 7, Martha T. 48, Mary E. 48, Meriwether 48, Pamelia 48, Ro. R. 48, Roger 6, Wm A.48, LIGHTFOOT: Nancy 49, Walker 32, Wm 32, 49; LINDSEY: John 6, Orlanzo,42; LIPSCOMBE: Capt. Ambrose 63, Betty 42, 49; LIPSCOMB 61, James H.49, LOCKHART: Samuel 7; LYON: William.

McCARTY: Loudon 7; McGhee; Jos. F. 21, Elmira 21; McKENZIE: Ben.25, Susan A. B. 25; MACON: Sarah 13, Thomas 60, 62, Wm.H. 8,57,59,60,61, 62; MADISON: John 55, Lucy A. 13, Wm.C. 13; MAHONE: Richard 7, MANNING (and. MANNIN): Armistead 8, Richard 8, Armistead, R. 44; MARSHALL: Col.61, Frances.59, J.58, OTWAY P.25; MARSTON: Eliz.B.23,Mary F.31,Wm.W. 31; MARTIN: Alcesta,34, Alice 7, Angelina 13,Betsy 41,Caleb 7, Cordelia 19, Dandridge 7, 55, Eliza 55, Elizabeth 20, 7, Eliz C.20,Ellyson 7, Elvira 13, Ferdinand,D.20, Frances 41,50, Harriet 20,34, Isabella 13, James 8, James B.50, James H.20, John 55, John C. 50, John B. 7, Joshua 7,8,Julius 7,55, Julius Jr.7,Major 13, Martha A.W. 19, Mary 38, Mary E. 19, Perks, 58, Parke,F.20,Patsey 20, Philany A. 13, Robert 13, R.M.20, Ro. S. 19, Susan 41,Thomas 20, Thos.S. 34, Virginia 20, 34, William 34, Wm.8, Wm.A. 13,William B.7, William E. 19; MASON: Cath.16, John 7, Ro.M. 16,Sarah 14,Thos.B. 16; MASSIE: Anne 8, Hugh 8, John 8, Wm 7, MAZARET: Maj. 61, MEANLEY or MENNLEY: Ann M. 53, Cordelia W. 53, Elizabeth 7 Emeline E. 41,Geo M.53, James A.25, John P.53, Maria L.53, Sarah H. 53; MEEKINS: Christmas 7,David 7,Isaac 7, Joseph 7, Ned.7; MENNIN: Richardson 7, William 7; MERCER: Elizabeth 8, MEREDITH: Ann E. 15, Edw. P. 14,15, Eliza 33, Emiley 15, Hannah 33, Henry 15, Jos T. 15, Mary 15,Robert 15, Ro.F.33, Saml.A. 33, Selina P. 15, Susan B.23,Thos. 15, Wm.A. 15, Winston 15; MERRY(or MARRY) Ann Ann 46, Jno.L, 45, Joice 46, Wm B.46, William (Marry) 8; MERRIMAN: Frances E.

15, Geo.S. 15, Jane 15, Jno T. 26, Martha I. 15,26, Nancy 27, Richard G. 16, Sarah A. 15, Thomas 8, Wm.T. 16; MEAUX: Hubbard R. 7, Thomas 7, MILLER: Christopher 8; MILLS: Archer W. 41, Betty 41, Cynthia E. 35, Eliz T. 40, Emiley A. 35, Eugenie C. 41, Fleming 54, Frances T. 41, Jane 35, John 8, Jno A. 35, Mansfield 40, Martha 41, Martha J.40, Mary E. 35, Virginia 40, Wm H.41, Wm P. 41, Wm P. 41, MINOR: Ann 13, George C. 13, Henry C. 13, Joseph 13, Thomas H. 13; MITCHELL: Abner 55, Archer R. 31, Eliza W. 31, Geo.W. 31, James M. 31, James R. 55, John E. 31, Jno G. 31, John R. 55, Joice P. 55, Lucius E. 55, Martha 31, Mary 31, Peter G. 31, Sarah C. 31, Sarah S. 31, Susan M. 55, Wm. A. 31, MOODY: Eliz. D. 22, Harriet W. 22, Maria A. 22, Martha 22, Martha A. 22, Mary W. 22, Saml. M.22, Sarah I.22. Thos. 7, Thomas I. 22, MOON: Christopher 7, MOORE: Ann E. 41, Barnett 43, Berned 7, Elizabeth 28, Fanny 41, John 28, John ... 28 Judith 43, Margaret 29, Raleigh P.28, Wm 7; MORRISS: Agness 52, Anna F. 31, Betty T. 52, Daniel 7, David S.M. 31, Florence E. 50, Geo.W. 31, Irena 52, John 8, John C. 8, Jos.C.40, Lucy L.50, Lucy A. 49, Mary A. 41, Patrickanna 40, Rebecca 31, Richard 52, Richd. Jr. 52, Thomas 7, Tho. J. 52, Thos.S. Jr. 49, Thos. S. Sr. 41, Wm Henry 52, Wm N.31; Morgan: Edward T. 24, Jane 7, Jane P. 23, Laura I. 24, Lucenia N.24, Wm.I.23, Wm.P.24, MOSS: Betty F.23, Elizabeth 62, George 7, Harriet M.23, Judith 7, Julius 7, Mary 22, Reuben 23, Reubenette 23 23, Samuel 7, 60,62, Samuel Jr.7, Ro.I.23 Susan B.23, Susan W. 23, William 7, MOUNTCASTLE: Vernon 52, MUHLENBURG: Gen. 58, 61, Mullen: Celia 30, John 53, John (Mullin) 7, John H.30, MUSE: Nelson 49, MUTLOW: Zachariah 8.

NELSON: Frances 48, Gen. 57, 59, 60 61, Letitia R. 48, Mary S. 13, Philip M. 48, Sally B.48, Wm. P. 48; NERO: Frances 16, Naomi 16.

OAKLEY: Fleming 53, James 8, James A. 53, Louisa 53, Martha 53, Wm.T. 53; ODELL: Elizabeth 39, Henry H.39, Jno.D. 39, Margaret D. 39 Sarah F. 39, Thos. M.39, OSBORNE: Squire 8; OTEY: Ann K.C.42, Anna 42, Betty 54, Elizabeth 8, Isaac 8, 54, James 8, James A. 38, James G.38, John 42, Lucy A. 38, Martha 54, Martha R. 38, Mary 38, Marye Anne 8, Sarah 38, Sarah W. 38, Wm R. 38, OTTER: John G. 8; OWEN: William 8.

PAGE: Thomas M. 13; PARKE: Edmund 8, John 50; PARKER: Col. Richard 59; PARKINSON: Ann E. 48, Albert T. 48, C.D. 24, Edmonia C.48, Elizabeth 8, Ellen A.24, Hannah D. 24, James F. 24, Jno.F. 48, Jordan C. 48, Joseph 8, Jos.W. 24, Joshua 8, 48, Mary E.24, Wm.8, Wm A. 24; PARRISH: Amanda S. 18, Ann E. 18, Geo. I. 18, James 30, John 9, 17, John B. 18, Marcus A A. 18, Mary E. 18, Mary R. 30, Minerva,D. 17, Wm 9, Wm F. 17, PARSONS: Hopewell,8; PATTERSON: Alice C. 13, Dand.47, Jesse 8, John B. 13, Jno. T. 13, Margaret 39, Margaret S. 39, Mary I. 13; PATTEY 9, PEACE: Alonzo 21, Joseph I. 21, Julia 21, Roselin 21; PEARMAN: John 47; PEARSON: Betty 16, Charles 16, Chas.G.52, Elizabeth 16, Lucy C. 52, Mary 16, Robinette 16, Sarah 16, Sarah E. 52, Wm.G. 52, PEERMAN: Thomas 8; PERGE: Jacob 8; PERKINS: Fanny P. 47, Ro. 61, Robert 9, Philabes: Edward 8, PHILLIPS: Elizabeth 15, James W. 15, Jane 15, Julius 8, Richard 15; PIERCE: John P. 54; PLEASANTS: J.W. 58, PLEMENT: Thomas 8; POINDEXTER: Agnes C. 52, Edwin P. 52, Frances P. 52, Geo.W. 52, Martha C. 47, Mary 47, Mary E. 52, M.A. 47, M.E. 47, J.L. 47, J.L. Jr. 47, John L. 58,59,60, 63,John S. 9, Judith 9, LaFayette W. 52, Lightfoot, 8, Polly 8, Susan 9, Susan W. 52, Willis L.52; POLLARD: Alice C. 17, Anne 9, Fielding 8, John 8, John S. 17, Pleasant 8, Robert 8, 61,63,64,Ro.I.17 Ro.S. 17, Sarah M.17, Susanna 64; PROOVO: Alex. 53, Ann A. 53, Margaret 53,; POMFREY: Ann E. 55, Betsy 46, Betty 27, Cath 53, Eliz. S.27, Elvira 55,27, Frances E. 55, Geo. M. 55, James P. 53, Major. A. 55, Mary 55, Mary S. 27,

G.

Margaret A. 55, Mildred 8, Pleasant 9, Wm. 8, Wm. A. 55, Wm. P. 27; **POND:** Debora 24, Emeline W. 36, Frances 36, Henry L. 36; | POORHOUSE 9, 55); **PORTER:** Dianna 38, Elizabeth 41, James 8, James H. 38, John 8, Jno. R.T. 39, **PORTERFIELD:** Colo. 57, **PRICE:** Betty S. 51, Capt. John 63, Lurina P. 51, Mary B. 51, Prudence Primrose, 51, Wm. 57.

QUARLES: Capt. Henry 60, 61, Capt James 61, **QUIGGEN:** Susanna 9,

RAGLAND: Dick 9, George 9; **RAGDALE:** Major 57, 59, 61, **RAINBOW:** Ned. 9; **RATCLIFF:** Adeline 37, Benj. H. 23, Cath.E. 32, Cornelia 23, Geo. T. 23, Harriet P. 23, John 23, Judith W. 35, Lucy A. 35, Lydia 37, Martha A. 35, Mary A. 35, Nancy 37, Olivia E. 23, Thomas 9, William 9, 35, 63; **REDWOOD:** John 9; **RICHARDSON:** Adeline 30, Addison F. 29, Alva S. 30, And. P. 32, Ange T. 32, Ann E. 29, Aug. 32, Colo. 60,62,Colus. 32, David 29, Edmund 9,46, Eliz. 30, Eliz. A. 53, Geo.N.36,Geo.W. 32, Harriet 29, Harriet B. 29, Holt 9, James 29,30, James A. 46, James L. 30, Jno. A. 36, Jno. M. 29, Jno. W. 30, John 9, Joseph O. 29, Louisa 30, Margaret A. 29, Martha 32, Mary A. 30,31, Mary G. 30, Mary H. 32, Octavia 32, Senora 29, Susan 32, Sylvester, H. 32, Capt. Thomas 63, Thee. 32, Turner 9,29, Wm. 9,30,32 32,57,Wm. A. 29, Wm H 58, Wm P.53; **RICHESON:** Colo.Holt; **ROACH:** Chs; 44. Martha 44; **ROBBINS:** Benj. 30, Daniel 30, Eliz. 30, Harriet 30, James 32, Joseph 30, Mary 31, Sarah 30, Thomas 30, Wm.Robbins,30, ROBERTS: James 9, **ROBERTSON:** Isabella 54, Robert 9, **ROPER:** Eldridge 9, John 9, Julia 35, Louisa M. 17, Ro.R. 17, Wm 9, Wm. H. 17, Ross; Jane 9, Warren 47, Wm 9, Wm P 49, **ROYSTER:** Elizabeth 23, Ellen,23, Harriet 23, Jno. W. 51, Lawrence 23, Lucy C. 51, Susan B. 23, **RUSSEL:** Armistead 9, William 9.

SAMPLE: Parson 60, **SANSENN:** Mary F. 50; **SANSUM:** Sarah 49; **SAUNDERS** (SAUNDERS): Edmund, 45, George 9, Isaac 9, John 10, Julius 9, Ro. A 45; **SAVAGE:** Ann. S. 19, Eliz. A. 21, Harriet 22, Maria P.21, Mary E. 21, Nathaniel L. (Judge) 60, Nathan L. 21, Norton R. 21, Sarah E. 21, Southy 9, Southey L.21, Wm. A F. 21, Wm.R. 19, Wm W. 19; SCOT: Col.59, **SHACKLEFORD:** Andrew 42, Emeline 42, John 42, Lewellen 42, Mary 42, Richard 42, Ro. Leo 42, Susan 42, Wm.H. 42, Zac. 42, **SHELL:** Fanny 9, **SHERMAN:** Ann C. 17, Ballard, 9, 42, Eliza D. 45, Eliza J.42, Eliz. W. 43, Henley B.45, Henry M. 51, James T. 17, Lucinda H.42, Mary 30, Michael 10, 51,Nancy 17- Ro. M. 43, Sarah V. 51, Tho. B. 45, Wm.M. 43; **Silliman:** Rev. Jonathan 59; **SLATER:** Daniel 9, Edward 62, Ellen B.53, **SMILEY** W. 53, Fluvanna P. 53, Henly 10, John 53, John S. 53, Leonard A. 53, Martha A. 53, Mary 9, Selden C. 32, Virga. W. 53, Wm. 9,59, 60, **SLAUGHTER:** Joe. 15; **SMITH:** Anne 9, Charles 10,39, Ellen 39, Eliza 14,Gregory(Col) 61, Henry 14, Henry L. 14, James 39, James A. 46, John 10, John T. 46, Mary B. 14, Ro. 39,Ro.F. 61,Sally 39, Wm 9, Wm.M.46; **SMITHY:** Casander 9, George 23, Lucy M.23,Pleasant T.23,Polly 9, Wm.M.Smithie 23; **SNEED:** Sally 9; **SOLE:** Sally 9; **SOUTHALL:** Emeline S. 40, Maria 51; **SPICER:** Joseph 64; **SPILLER:** Capt. Benj.C. 63; **SPRAGGINS:** Mary 9; **STAMPER:** James 50, James Jr. 50, John 50, Martha J.50, Octavia E. 50; **STANLEY:** Capt.John 63, **STARK:** Betty W. 54; **STEVENS:** Gen. 59, **STEWARD:** John 9, Lacy 9, Thomas 9, Thomas S. 9, **STEWART:** Ann E. 34, Christiana 37, GEORGE 40, Indiananna 43, James A. 37, Jno.B.43. Josephine 34, Julia A.37, Mary E.34,Mary F.43,Maria L.34,Rebecca 37, Richard 37, Ro.F.34,Sarah 37,43, Wyatt 37, **STIFF:** Susanna 9, Stith: Mary 45, **STREET:** Parke 64, **STROUD:** Eliz. 43; **SULLIVAN:** Eugene 33, SUTTON: F.V. 60; **SWEENEY:** Chas.H.35, Elizabeth 9, Eliza F.4 40, Eliz. U.34, Jno.M.34, Jonathan 9, Jos.C.40, Jos.W. 35, Maria L.35, Martha 34, Minerva 40,Mary F.35, Richardson F.34,Sarah 34, Stephen B. 35, Wm.T. 39.

H.

TALIMAN: John 10, TALLY: Fleming C. 10, James W. 51, Lucy A. 41, Nathaniel C. 41, Nicholas 10, Richd. W. 41, Wm.C. 41, TANDY: Elizabeth 10, John 10; TAYLOR: A. 36, Abner 36, Ann E. 51, Ann M. 23, Col.60,62, Clemens. 10. Edwrd.H. 50, Elizabeth 36, Eliz. 39, Geo. W. 50, 51, James 10, 36, James.R.30, James T. 50, John 39, Jno. A. 57, John Augustine 61,62, Littleberry W. 50, Martha 39, Martha A. 51, Martha M.39, Mary 10, Mary E. 51, Orina 50, Richd.B. 41, Richardson 10, Ro. S. 41, Sally 10, Saml. C. 50, Saml. T. 50, Susan 39, Susan B. 36, Talsey 10, William 10, Wm.R. 10, Zachary 50; (TAVERN, 23, 54); TERRELL: Allen A. 19, Ann E. 21, Ann H. 55, Ara A. 19, Arthur C. 55, Betsey 20, Caroline A. 22, Casandra 19, Cornelia 20, Delia A. 19, Eliz.A 19, Frances A.20, Geo. A. 21, Geo. P.55, Henry C. 21, Joseph C. 19, Leigh R. 55, Littleberry,19, Laurena 19, Martha 20, Mertha D. 21, Parthena 20, Richmond H. 23, Ro. C. 20,21, Thos. H. 21, 55, 57, 61,62, Virginia 20, Wash F. 21, Wm. 10, 21, Wm. F. 23; TERREY: Patsy 23; THACKER: Sackville 64, THOMAS: Benj. A. 22; THOMPSON: Ann.E. 46, James 10, John 10, Jno. H. 46, Mary 46, Mary F. 46, Polly 10, Rebecca W. 46 46; TIMBERLAKE: Benj. 10, 36, Benj. N. 36, Courtney T. 36, David 37, Edgar 25, Eliza 26, Eliza 37, Eliz.P.26, Eliza S. 36, Eliza T. 36, Elija.F.37, Frances 50, Frances H. 36, Geo.A. 36, Haman 37, Harriet A. 50, James W. 26, James A. 36, Jas. B.36, Jas.P. 50, Jane 45, John 10, Jno.50, Jno.C.36, Jno.H.35, Jno.M.25, Jno.T.50, Josephine 25, Maria L.50, Martha 45, Margt.W.38, Mary 37, 45,Mary E. 36, Mary T. 50, Melville F.26, Richard 10, Richd.M.39, Sally 26, Sally H.45, Sarah F. 26, Thomas 50, Th.N. Jr. 50, Virga.C.36, Warren 45, Wm.45,Wm.I.36, TOK: Capt. 63, TOLER: Henrietta 49, Henry 49, Susan 49; TRIMMIER: James H. 18, Mary 18, Thos. L. 18, Wm.F. 18; TUCKER: Ann E. 54, Archer 54, Elizabeth 20, George 20, James D. 53, John (Agt) 23, Martha 54, Martha C. 53, Mary F.53, Miles, 10, 52,54, Richard A.20, Richd. 54, Sarah J.53; TURNER: Cath. 19, Charles 10, Edmund P.44, Emily F. 19, John D. 44, John P.44, Louisa B.44, Lucy 25, Mary E. 19, Nath'l. I.25, Octavia A. 19, Robert 10,Ro.E. 19, Ro.T.19, Susanna 10, Susan V. 19, Thos. I.25, Thom. J. 61, William 19, 53; TROWER: Lucy 10, TUNSTALL: Alice 16, Ann E. 16, Eliza 16, Frances A. 14,Martha.C. 16,Miles C. 16, Thomas 10, Thomas C. 14, Thos.R. 16, William R. 14, TWINNEY: John 10: TYLER: Caroline 51, David 17, Hezekiah 51, Hon. John 59, 63, TYREE: Alonzo 26, Augusta 26, Batts 10, Benj. 45, Betsey 26,45, Christianna 26, Cyrus 45, Dickey 10, Elizabeth 10, Eliza A. 36, Francis 10, George 45, Harriet 26, Henry 10, Isaac 13,James 10,45 James A. 29, Jno.C. 36, Leonidas R. 36, Maria 26, Marion 45, Mary 10, Nancy 45, Patsy 45, Richard 10, Richd. 45, Thomas 10, Sheppard 26, Wm.45, William 10,26, Wm.C. 36, Wilson J.26,

VAIDEN: Albert H. 44, Algernon 29, Aspesia 44, Benj.32, Caroline 54, Cynthia 54, Edward I.29, Eliza 42, Elizabeth 10, Elizabeth Jr. 10, Fluvanna S. 14, Galba 44, H.D. 29, Henry 10, Isaac 10,43, 54, Isaac H.54, Lieut.Jacob 60, 62, James 50, Jeremiah 10, John B. 18, John B. 44, John H. 15, Judith T. 18,43,Judith E. 43, Lucy). 29, Margaret 42, Martha 42, Mary E. 54, Mary Jane 14 14, Mary L.44, Melville 44, Micajah 10,Otelia 42, Rebecca 18, Sarah M. 14,29, Susan C. 54, Susan V. 14,Thomas 10, Virgillia 42, Vulosco 44, William H. 42, 54, Wm H. Sr. 14; VALENTINE: Joseph 10; VAUGHAN: Ann.M. 10, Elizabeth 34, Eleanor,38, Henry 10, John M.49, Jno.T. 38, Maria A. 10,Pryor 10,Roscoe,T. 38, Sarah M.38, Susan E. 38, William 49, Wm.H.49, Wm.R.38,

WADDEL: Mary 11,Elizabeth 11; WADE: Ann 19, Ann E. 34, Betsey 27, Betty C. 46, Cath.M.34, Dabney 18, David 11, 19, Dics,18, Gideon 11,13,Gid. D. 46, Georgianna 14,Jas.H.34, Joseph 17, Maria D. 34, Martha 18, Martin 11, 19, Mary S. W. 34, Pleasant 11, Ro.W. 34, Sarah 27, Susan I. 14, William C. 15, Wm.D.C. 34, Wm.T. 34; WALKER: Benj H. 43, David 11, Fanny B. 43, Florence 11, Morman B.43, Jas. D. 43, Jno.H.37, Lucy R. 37, Mary A.43, Mary B. 43,Ro. H. 43 WALLS: Elizabeth 11,Emiley 43, James 43, Lornitta 43, Martha A.E. 47,

Mary 43, Richard 11, Ro. 43, Thomas 11, Victoria 49, Wm.T. 49, WARING:
Jno. W.55, Maria E. 55, Mary E. L. 55, Payne 55, Ro.L.55, Thos. B. 55, Wm.H.
55, Wm. P. 55; WARNER: Ann. 55, James 55, John 11, Jno. 55, Louisiana 55;
WARREN: Eliz. C. 51, Eliz. L. 52, Eliza M. 51, Geo.W. 51, John 11, Jno.H. 52
Nancy C. 51, Robert 57, Ro. 60, Sarah J. 52, WASHINGTON: Gen. 59, Watkins:
John D. 11, P.C. 54; WEBB: Conrad, 11, George 11, Henry 13, John H. 57,
John S. 11, 58, 59, Lewis 11, Mary A. 13, Samuel 15; WELSH: Maj. 59, WHITCOMB
Rebecca 11; WHITE: Jos. 22, Nathaniel 11; WICKER: Bentley 19, John 19,
Joseph 19, Joshua 15, Martha 19, William 19; WILKES: Abner 37, Chs. T. 37,
George 34, John 11, Louisianna 38, Martha E. 37, Mary R. 37, Rebecca 38,
Reuben 11, Richard S. 34, Sarah A. 34, Selden 38, William 34; WILKINS: James
11, 43, 64, John 11, Ro.C.43, Sarah 43; WILKINSON: Frances E. 41, George
(lawyer) 11, James 11, James P. 11, Leonidas A. 17, Lucy A. 41, Maria 54,
Nancy 41, Roseann 17, Sarah 11, Susanna 11, Thomas 17, Wm. C. 17; WILLIAMS:
Alexander 40, Augustua 35, Bartlet, 11, Ben.W. 26, Caroline 40, Cynthia 28,
David 11,30, Delilah 26, Dianer 62, Dudley 11,26, Edward 40, Ellen H. 32,
Foster 62, Harriet 26, 47, Hugh 47, Isham 26, James 11, 60, 61, 62, James A.35,
John 28, 61, 62, Jno.B. 55, Josiah 62, Leroy 32, 62, Lucy 62, Mary A. 26,
Meredith 11, Minerva 28, Mortimer 35, Nancy 26, Octavia S. 35, Patsey 28,
Pattey 61,62, Richmond 61, 62, Sarah A.28, Susan 32, Susan A. 26, Virginia
35, William H. 11, Wm.D. 40, Wilson 61,62, WILLIAMSON: Mary A. 54, Geo.54;
WILLIS: William 11, WINFREY: Austin 11, Major 11, Thos C. 45, William 11;
WINSTON: Philip B. 64; 64; WOOD: John 27; WOODRAM: John 11; WOODWARD: Ann.E.
37, Augustus 16, Averilla 41, Barsha 50, Bartlet 11, Cath. 52, Ellen 25, Eliz.
37, Frances 26,34, Geo.P. 53, Harman 37, Henry 11, Jno.F. 34, Joseph 11, Jos.H.
34, Lemuel 37, Martha 11, 25,26,34, Mary 37, Mary A. 16,25, Mary A.B. 25,
Micaj. 45, Minerva 34, Nancy 34, Nancy J.52, Philn. 52, Richard G. 34,
Richmond 11, Rob rt 37, Sally 45, Susan 52, Theo.H. 16, Virginia 34, War.M.
25, Warwick (Wawick)? 11, Wesley 45, Wm.34, Wm.H.37, Wyatt F. 26, Wyatt S.
25; WRIGHT: Cath. 48, Eliz. 22, Henry 11, Henry T. 22, John 28, 50, Jno. A.22
Joseph 50, Judith 11, Martha A.22, 50, Martha J. 50, Mary 22, Mary T. 48,
Mary A. E. T. 41, Pleasant 22, Richard 11, 15, 63, Ro.B. 41, Sam'l,C. 30,
Sarah 31, 50, Thos, 22, 41, 48, Wm.D. 50, Wm. Jos. 22; WYATT: John 11.

    YATES: Richard 11; YOUNG   James 11, William H. 11.

BIBLIOGRAPHY.

Other available published material on New Kent County, Virginia.

    CROZIER'S Va. County Records, Vol. 6, pp 205, 268-- gives a partial list of New Kent Land Grants.

    HARDESTY'S Historical and Geographical Encyc., Virginia edition, pp 396-401; 418-422, gives biographical sketches.

    TYLER'S Quarterly Magazine, Vol. 1, p. 52-57, gives "Tombstones in New Kent Co. Vol. 10, p. 177, gives a partial list of "Military Classes in 1782" of New Kent Co.
                         Vol. 12, p 194, gives a few "Epitaphs of New Kent County."

    VIRGINIA Tax lists of 1782 to 5, pp 92 & 93, -gives New Kent Co. This is published by Government Printing Office, Wash. 1908.

    VESTRYBOOK of St. Peter's, New Kent Co., p 242. A volume of the "Parish Record Series", no. 3, Published 1905.

    VESTRYBOOK OF Blisland Parish, New Kent & James City Cos., Va., from 1721 to 1786, by C. C. Chamberlayne. Richmond 1935.

    PARISH REGISTER, of St. Peter's New Kent Co., Va., from 1680 to 1787. Pub. 1904.

www.ingramcontent.com/pod-product-compliance
Lightning Source LLC
Chambersburg PA
CBHW020702300426
44112CB00007B/487